RADIX LISTENING for the TOEFL iBT®

BLUE LABEL

1

RADIX LISTENING FOR THE TOEFL iBT®: BLUE LABEL 1

Series editor	Ji Hyun Kim
Project editors	Yuram Jo, Yeonsue Choi, Hyejin Kim
Contributing writers	Bryce Olk, Nathaniel Galletta, Tamar Harrington, Michael Ledezma, MyAn Le
Design	dots
Editorial designers	In-sun Lee
Photo Credits	www.shutterstock.com

www.neungyule.com

TABLE OF **CONTENTS**

INTRODUCTION

TOEFL®: Test of English as a Foreign Language

The TOEFL is a standardized test developed to assess English language proficiency in an academic setting. By achieving a high score on the TOEFL, you will demonstrate that your skills in English qualify you for admission to a college or university where English is used as the language of instruction. Academic institutions around the world will look at your performance on the TOEFL, so whether you are hoping to study in North America, Australia, Europe, or Asia, this test is the key to your future educational career.

TOEFL Today: TOEFL iBT

The TOEFL Internet-based test (iBT) is the version currently administered in secure testing centers worldwide. It tests reading, listening and writing proficiency, and speaking abilities.

Getting to Know the TOEFL iBT: Test Format

You will take all four sections of the test (Reading, Listening, Speaking, and Writing) on the same day. The duration of the entire test is about four hours.

Test Section	Description of Tasks	Timing
Reading	3–4 passages, each approximately 700 words 10 questions on each passage	54–72 minutes
Listening	3-4 lectures, each 3-5 minutes long 6 questions per lecture 2–3 conversations, each around 3 minutes long 5 questions per conversation	41–57 minutes
BREAK		10 minutes
Speaking	4 tasks • 1 independent task – speak about personal knowledge and experience • 3 integrated tasks – read-listen-speak / listen-speak	17 minutes
Writing	2 tasks • 1 independent task – write about personal knowledge and experience • 1 integrated task – read-listen-write	50 minutes

Score Scales

You will receive a score between 0 and 30 for each section of the test. Your total score is the sum of these four scores and will be between 0 and 120.

Registering for the TOEFL iBT

The most convenient way to register to take the TOEFL iBT is online by visiting the "Register for the TOEFL® Test" section of the TOEFL website (www.ets.org/toefl). Here, you can check current listings of testing centers and schedules. It is also possible to register for the test by phone and by mail. For more information, consult the TOEFL iBT Bulletin, which can be downloaded or ordered from the TOEFL website. It is free and features important information regarding the registration process.

GUIDE TO LISTENING

The Listening section of the TOEFL iBT will require you to demonstrate your understanding of English as it is spoken in academic settings in North America and throughout the world.

Listening Section Content

The material you will hear in the Listening section will include academic lectures typical of a classroom setting and conversations related to student life. The speech will accurately reflect real-life spoken English and may include the following features: polite interruptions, mistakes, and corrections, hesitations and repetitions. Although many of the speakers in the Listening section will have standard American accents, some may have a regional U.S. accent or an accent from another English-speaking country.

Academic Lectures

There are two formats of academic lectures that appear in the Listening section: monologues and interactive lectures. In a monologue, the professor is the only one who speaks. In an interactive lecture, one or two students will participate in discussion with the professor about the information he or she is presenting.

Conversations

Unlike the lectures, the conversations in the TOEFL iBT do not involve specific academic material. Instead, they are concerned with problems and situations typical of student life. One speaker is usually a student, and the other can be a professor, teaching assistant, office clerk, librarian, another student, etc.

Types of Questions

The questions found in the Listening section can be divided into 7 categories.

Question Type	Testing Point
Main Idea	The overall content or purpose of the lecture or conversation
Detail	Important details introduced in the lecture or conversation
Function	The speaker's reason for making a specific statement in the lecture or conversation
Attitude	The speaker's attitude toward or degree of certainty about ideas in the lecture or conversation
Organization	The overall relationship between major ideas in the lecture
Connecting Content	Relationships that have been stated or clearly implied in the lecture or conversation
Inference	The speaker's intended meaning or implication in the lecture or conversation

Important Points to Keep in Mind

≫ You can take notes on all of the listening materials as you hear them. This is recommended, as you are not expected to memorize the material you hear.

≫ There will be a picture or pictures shown on the computer screen to provide context for each lecture or conversation.

≫ For lectures that use specialized terms, the new vocabulary may appear on a "blackboard screen" on the computer. This imitates the way a professor might write important terms on a blackboard. The purpose of these screens is to assist in your understanding of the lecture, but they do not necessarily present information related to the questions you will have to answer.

≫ When you see a headphone icon next to a question, it means you will have to listen again to an excerpt from the lecture or conversation before answering the question.

≫ There is no time limit for individual questions in the Listening section, but you must budget your time in order to finish the entire section within the allotted 41-57 minutes.

≫ A toolbar is displayed on the computer screen. It lists the section and question number you are currently working on, the amount of time remaining, and has help, navigational, and volume buttons.
Keep in mind that in the Listening section, you cannot return to a question after you have confirmed your answer.

Tactics for the TOEFL iBT Listening Section

To strengthen your listening skills before taking the TOEFL iBT, it is essential to frequently expose yourself to sources of spoken English. Watching movies and television and listening to radio programs on various topics are simple and effective ways of doing this. To receive practice specifically with academic speech, check out the audio material available at libraries and bookstores. You may find it helpful to obtain a transcript of the material so you can read along as you listen.

During the test, remember to:
- make a note of new words and concepts that are presented in the lectures
- remain focused by thinking about what the speakers will likely say next
- consider each speaker's motivation and why they present certain information
- concentrate on the organization of the lecture or conversation so you can notice the difference between changes in topic and digressions
- listen for keywords that demonstrate how important ideas are related to each other

HOW TO USE THIS BOOK

This book gives you instruction, practice, and strategies for performing well on the TOEFL iBT Listening Section. It will familiarize you with the appearance and format of the TOEFL iBT and help you prepare for the TOEFL test efficiently.

Each unit in the book corresponds to one of the seven question types in the Listening Section. Each unit consists of the following:
- An **Introduction** that provides basic information about the question type
- **Basic Drills** that offer short listening materials to give examples of the question type being covered and allow you to become familiar with it
- **Listening Practice** involving longer listening materials that will improve essential skills
- **iBT Practice** that provides extensive exercises
- **Note-Takings** that help you practice and improve note-taking skills for the TOEFL iBT
- **Dictations** that require a focus on accuracy, general comprehension, and special features of pronunciation while you transcribe or orally reproduce what you hear
- A **Vocabulary Review** that offers a variety of activities designed to help you review and master essential vocabulary

In addition, this book contains three **Actual Practice Tests** to help you measure your progress, and these appear after units 2, 4, and 7.

NOTE-TAKING STRATEGIES

In the TOEFL iBT Listening section, the lectures and conversations are 3-5 minutes long (about 500-800 words) and 3 minutes long (about 12-25 pairs) each. The Listening section does not test your faculty of memory but your understanding of listening materials. Thus, it is important to improve your note-taking skills for comprehensive listening. Here is how to take note effectively during the TOEFL iBT Listening test.

How to Take Conversation Notes

1. Find out the place the conversation takes place and the relationship between speakers

When understanding the conversation in the TOEFL iBT Listening section, it is helpful to perceive the context in which the conversation takes place. It is also helpful to divide your note into two parts (e.g., a student part & a professor part). For that reason, you should be careful not to miss the beginning part of the conversation.

2. Focus on the beginning part of the conversation

If not grasping the purpose of the conversation, you would be confused during the conversation. To know the conversation's outline, you should concentrate on the beginning part of the conversation and write down the purpose for which the interaction occurs and the problem or the complaint which initiates the conversation.

3. Write down the list of solutions or what to do

After jotting down the purpose of the conversation or the problem of one speaker, you should find out the solutions and advice from the other speaker. You probably would hear a couple of solutions and answers from the other party. Since there is a multiple-choice question with more than one answer in the TOEFL iBT Listening section, you should be prepared to make the list of the solutions.

4. Don't try to write down every word of the conversation

In conversation listening, it is most important to know why the conversation takes place and what the solutions are. Some people are too careful at taking notes during listening and miss some crucial parts to answer the questions. To avoid it, you should make your note brief and neat by skipping determiners, connecting words and pronouns, or using abbreviations. Here are commonly used symbols in fast note-taking:

Symbol	Meaning	Symbol	Meaning
=	equal	#	number
x	times	w/	with
w/o	without	w/in	within
⇨	results in	⇦	comes from
>	greater, more than	<	less, smaller than
+	plus	–	minus

Student: Sorry, I'm late. I had a printer problem.

Professor: Don't worry about it. I know how troublesome printers can be. So, you wanted to talk to me about your paper?

S: Right. I've decided on a topic, but I don't know where to begin. I want to write about Evolution vs. Creationism. I've done a lot of research on both sides, and I have a lot to say... but I'm just having trouble figuring out how to start.

P: Okay, what you need to do before you try to write the paper is to make an outline. Organization is so important when writing a paper. If you write an outline first, it will help you stay organized. That way, you won't get off topic.

S: An outline? Is that the same thing as a road map?

P: No, they're similar, but the difference is that a road map presents different paths you could take. It could be useful when you set every possible plan or guideline for a goal, but when it comes down to writing the paper, you really need an outline.

S: I see.

P: And there's one more thing I want to emphasize. When writing papers for any class, try to be creative. We, professors, get so bored reading virtually the same paper over and over again. If your paper stands out from the rest, it makes it more enjoyable to read and, providing everything else is okay, you'll probably get a better grade. So, be creative by... um by approaching your topic from new perspectives.

S: I'll keep that in mind. Thanks.

📋 **NOTE-TAKING**

* Topic: talk about the paper
  Problem: did research but don't know how to start

  Advice 1: Write an outline first to stay organized
  Q. outline = road map?
  ⇨ No. Road map = show many ways
                     useful when setting many plans

  Advice 2: To be creative

How to Take Lecture Notes

1. Listen carefully to the introduction and write down the keywords

Regarding lectures, keywords appear in the introduction in general. The lecturer does not start his/her lecture without letting students be prepared for the lecture. By knowing this outline, you will be better prepared to anticipate what notes you need to take.

2. Concentrate on and write down in accordance with two factors

The lectures in the TOEFL iBT Listening section deal with one specifi c topic. Most of the lectures in the Listening section include one topic sentence and several supporting details, evidence, or examples. Thus, you should divide your note into a topic sentence and supporting details.

3. Pay attention to signal words like "for example"

When lecturers give examples or supporting details, they start with signal words. You have to pay close attention to the signalized details. Here are some typical signal words used mainly in lectures: There are three reasons why…, First… Second… Third, On the other hand…, On the contrary…, In Contrast…, For example…, As an example…, For instance…, Similarly…, Further…, Furthermore….

4. Don't try to write down every word of the lecture

As previously stated in How to Take Conversation Notes, the 4th rule is also applied to the lecture. It is likely to miss some crucial information for taking notes too perfectly. Make your note brief and simple by using some symbols mentioned above and omitting minor specifications.

Script

Professor: Waste management is about all the processes from collection and transport to recycling or disposal of waste materials. The methods of each process vary widely between countries or regions, and today we're going to study a couple of those ways of waste management.

Let's start with the most common and traditional method of dealing with waste, the landfill. We simply gather up all of the garbage and take it to a spot designated for garbage — the landfill, also known as "the dump." We've been doing this since the dawn of cities. We find or create a large pit to keep all of our garbage in. The problem is, landfills generate pollution.

When it rains, the water reacts with elements of the landfill and proceeds to pollute the groundwater. Also, when organic material breaks down in a landfill, it gives off a gas called landfill gas. Landfill gas is mostly composed of methane and carbon dioxide, which is dangerous because it pollutes the air and contributes to global warming.

One way to reduce the amount of waste we put in landfills is to recycle. Items made from aluminum, glass, paper, and some plastics are commonly collected, and the materials are made into different products. Recycling efforts in recent years have significantly reduced the burden on landfills. Now, recycling programs are often said to be more expensive than other methods because of the cost of the collecting and sorting process. But when you think of environmental needs, the cost of recycling seems negligible. It surely reduces the amount of waste and, unlike landfill, doesn't emit harmful gas.

📋 NOTE-TAKING

* Waste Management
  = collection ~ recycling waste

1. Landfill (common & old)
   = gather and take it to the dump
   ⇨ Problem: polluting water & air (⇨ global warming)

2. Recycling
   = be made into different things
   ⇨ Problem: expensive
   But, good for environments!

PART

Basic Comprehension Questions

Main Idea

- Main Idea questions ask about the general idea of the conversation or lecture.
- You will need to understand what the conversation or lecture is mainly about.

QUESTION TYPES

1. Question forms for conversations
   - Why does the student go to see the professor?
   - What problem does the student have?
   - What are the speakers mainly discussing?

2. Question forms for lectures
   - What is the lecture mainly about?
   - What is the main point of the lecture?
   - What aspect of X does the professor mainly discuss?

BASIC DRILLS 01

1-1   What does the professor mainly talk about?

(A) Purposes of hibernation

(B) Seasons animals hibernate in

(C) Dangers to animals that are hibernating

(D) Differences between hibernation and sleep

1-2   Choose the sentence that is closest in meaning to what you hear.

(A) Animals need to save just as much energy in summer as in winter.

(B) Some types of animals must hibernate in hot weather, not cold weather.

2-1   What is the lecture mainly about?

(A) Ways to find meanings in paintings

(B) Various symbols in Van Gogh's work

(C) An analysis of a Van Gogh painting

(D) The influence of religion on Van Gogh's art

2-2   According to the professor, what do the following symbols mean?

(1) cypress: _____

(2) earth: _____

(3) sky: _____

Listen and fill in the blanks.

1.

Professor: Most people think that animals hibernate _____ _____ _____ and sleep through the winter. In fact, hibernation is a state where body functions are _____ _____ _____. To slow their metabolisms, hibernating animals _____ _____ _____ by 5 to 10 °C on average.

Animals hibernate for a few different reasons. First, hibernation is typically linked to seasonal changes that _____ _____ _____. Put simply, hibernation is a means of _____ _____. Of course, some animals hibernate in winter. But some animals have to _____ _____ _____ _____ _____. Recent studies have even suggested another reason: protection. When hibernating, animals do not move, make sounds, or produce smells. Therefore, they are hard _____ _____ _____ _____. So, as you can see, hibernation is not simply sleep.

2.

Professor: Let's move on to the next painting. The Starry Night is Van Gogh's most famous painting, and _____ _____ _____. It shows a night sky with stars and a quiet town with a church. Also, there are, umm... cypress trees _____ _____ _____, which are quite impressive.

Student: Do the cypress trees have _____ _____ _____?

P: Oh, yes. Some say that the cypress is _____ _____ _____ _____. In this painting, they are connecting earth and sky, which are symbols of humans and God. _____ _____ _____ _____ _____, the whole picture could have a religious meaning such as... um, perhaps our _____ _____ _____ God.

BASIC DRILLS 02

1-1 What is the lecture mainly about?

    Ⓐ What makes the Hubble Space Telescope effective

    Ⓑ Discoveries made with the Hubble Space Telescope

    Ⓒ Places where you can view space objects clearly

    Ⓓ The inventor of the first space telescope

1-2 Choose the sentence that is closest in meaning to what you hear. 🎧

    Ⓐ It is an unusual telescope which moves around the surface of the Earth.

    Ⓑ It is an unusual telescope which moves around the Earth in outer space.

2-1 What does the professor mainly discuss?

    Ⓐ Principles of economics

    Ⓑ How to spend your money smartly

    Ⓒ The reasons people should pay taxes

    Ⓓ What disposable income is

2-2 Choose the sentence that is closest in meaning to what you hear. 🎧

    Ⓐ In economics, the term 'disposable income' is commonly used.

    Ⓑ The term is often used to describe disposable income in economics.

Listen and fill in the blanks.

1.

Professor: Have you heard about the Hubble Space Telescope? It's a very special telescope which is _____ _____ _____ _____ _____. Many scientists think the Hubble is one of _____ _____ _____ telescopes. What I mean here _____ _____ is... the Hubble helps us to see space objects more clearly.

Student: Why is that? Does it have better lenses or something?

P: Maybe. But think about where it is. It is _____ _____ _____ while other telescopes are on the ground. The atmosphere blurs the view _____ _____ _____, so scientists can't see objects clearly with other telescopes. However, with the Hubble, scientists can _____ _____ _____ _____ of space objects.

2.

Professor: Disposable income is a standard term in economics. _____ _____ _____, but its meaning is really quite simple. Money _____ _____ _____ equals disposable income. This is _____ _____ _____. Let's say that you earn $100 per week, and you pay 20% in taxes — 20% of $100 is $20. This is what you will _____ _____ _____ _____ _____ to the government. Take your $100 weekly salary and _____ _____ _____ $20. The result is $80. Thus, $80 is what you have left from your weekly salary, _____ _____ _____. This is your disposable income.

LISTENING **PRACTICE 01**

SERVICE
ENCOUNTER

📋 **NOTE-TAKING**

Purpose: Look for _____ _____

• took a job in _____, but it doesn't _____ well

• need another job that offers _____ _____

   (even _____)

⇨ Let you know by _____ _____

1 **Why does the student go to the Career Center?**

   Ⓐ To advertise a job opening

   Ⓑ To complain about her present job

   Ⓒ To get information on part-time jobs

   Ⓓ To ask for a change in schedule

2 **Why does the student want to change her job?**

   Ⓐ Because she doesn't like her coworkers

   Ⓑ Because she's worried about her grades

   Ⓒ Because she'd rather work off-campus

   Ⓓ Because she wants to make more money

Listen and fill in the blanks.

Adviser: Hi. Welcome to the Career Center. Are you Stephanie?

Student: That's right. I _____ _____ _____ for 11 o'clock.

A: Of course. Have a seat. [pause] So what did you want to discuss today?

S: Well, I was interested in finding out about _____ _____ _____.

A: *[surprised]* Oh. Really?

S: Yes. Is there something wrong?

A: No... It's just that it's a little _____ _____ _____ _____ to be looking for a job. Most of the _____ _____ _____ _____ weeks ago.

S: Yes, I realize that. I actually _____ _____ _____ with the school library a couple of weeks ago. Unfortunately, it _____ _____ very well. I really need to earn more money.

A: I see. So you're planning to _____ _____ _____ _____?

S: Yes. I'd prefer to leave this job and find another that can offer me more money. I'd _____ _____ _____ _____ _____. I'd even work off-campus, if necessary.

A: All right, Stephanie. I'll look into what jobs are still available and _____ _____ _____ by tomorrow afternoon.

S: Thanks a lot.

LISTENING PRACTICE 02

MARKETING

📋 **NOTE-TAKING**

Products for _____, _____ groups

⇨ niche market

e.g. scissors for the _____

For success: meet the _____

e.g. computers for _____ vs. _____ _____

      (game, podcasting vs. office software)

1   What is the lecture mainly about?

     Ⓐ Basic rules for successful marketing

     Ⓑ Niche marketing and its principles

     Ⓒ The importance of product marketing

     Ⓓ Marketing strategies for niche markets

2   How do the products for a niche market differ from other products?

     Ⓐ They are usually sold online rather than offline.

     Ⓑ They will always make money for the company.

     Ⓒ They are products for left-handed people.

     Ⓓ They appeal only to special groups of people.

Listen and fill in the blanks.

Professor: Most products and services are designed for _____ _____ _____ people. But sometimes companies try to sell their products only to _____ _____, _____ _____. This special market is called a niche market. Let's see... _____ _____ _____ _____ are left-handed? [pause] When you use normal scissors, how does it feel?

Student: Not very good. I have to hold them _____ _____ _____ _____. It's uncomfortable to use my left hand.

P: That's right. Normal scissors are for right-handed people. However, there's a niche market — in this case, a market of _____ _____. If a company sells special scissors for these people, this is niche marketing. Niche products don't appeal to _____ _____ _____ people, but they still have _____ _____ _____, so they can earn money.

However, not every niche product earns money. For successful niche marketing, there's an important rule to _____ _____ _____: meet the needs of the market. If a company wants to produce a computer for young college students, their computers must _____ _____ _____ computers _____ _____ _____. They might have... um, maybe special software for online games and podcasting _____ _____ traditional office software.

LISTENING PRACTICE 03

PHYSICS

📋 **NOTE-TAKING**

How can _____ float on _____?

iceberg = ice cube

① Density: _____ > _____
            1kg/L   0.99kg/L

② Salinity of _____: salty → _____ density

1   **What does the professor mainly discuss?**

Ⓐ Why seawater has a high density

Ⓑ Why icebergs can float on water

Ⓒ How to measure the density of ice cubes

Ⓓ What causes water density to change

2   **What does the professor say about the characteristics of water?**
Click on 2 answers.

Ⓐ Water with high salinity has high density.

Ⓑ Seawater weighs less than icebergs.

Ⓒ Icebergs and ice cubes have different densities.

Ⓓ Water becomes less dense after it freezes.

Listen and fill in the blanks.

Professor: Have you ever wondered how it is possible for something _____ _____ _____ an iceberg to float on water? The answer is simple, in fact, if you think of an iceberg as _____ _____ _____ a really big ice cube. Ice cubes, of course, _____ _____ _____. This is because ice has a different density from water. So what does that mean? Let me _____ _____ _____ _____ — a liter of water weighs one kilogram, which means the density of water is one kilogram per liter. But _____ _____ _____ a liter of ice cubes, you'll find that they weigh 0.99 kilograms, making the density of ice cubes 0.99 kilograms per liter. So icebergs, _____ _____ _____ _____ _____ water, can float on water.

The salinity of seawater also _____ _____ _____. Salinity is a measure of _____ _____ _____ _____, and it affects water density. As you know, seawater is quite salty, and it has a high density, about, umm… 1.02 kilograms per liter. As a result, it is even easier for an iceberg to _____ _____ _____.

iBT PRACTICE

NOTE-TAKING

Otters

River otters	Sea otters
Live in many places	Live in _____
_____ face, _____ toes, _____ tails	Paws – paddle shape
Come onto _____	Spend most time in _____
_____ family _____ pups	_____ group _____ pup

1. What is the lecture mainly about?
   - (A) How to distinguish the two different kinds of otters
   - (B) The types of environments where otters live
   - (C) Why there are more sea otters than river otters
   - (D) The ways otters spend their time in water

2. What can be inferred about river otters regarding their habitats?
   - (A) Their habitats change depending on the time of the year.
   - (B) They can live almost anywhere, except where sea otters live.
   - (C) They have more habitats than suggested by their name.
   - (D) They sometimes fight with sea otters for their habitats.

3. Which of the following is NOT mentioned as a difference between river otters and sea otters?
   - (A) Body shape
   - (B) Diet
   - (C) Behavior
   - (D) Group size

Listen again to part of the lecture. Then answer the question.

4. Why does the professor say this: 🎧
   - (A) To have the students review the lecture
   - (B) To emphasize otters are not easy to see
   - (C) To change the topic of the lecture
   - (D) To introduce another difference

Listen and fill in the blanks.

Professor: Today we'll be talking about otters, class. And in North America, there are two types — river otters and sea otters. As you've _____ _____ _____, sea otters live in the ocean. Okay… well, it's not so easy with river otters… they don't just live in rivers. Uh… they're found near _____ _____ _____ _____… rivers, streams, lakes… but they also live in the sea _____ _____ _____. So river otters and sea otters can actually _____ _____ _____. And, well… this can make it hard _____ _____ _____ _____.

Luckily, though, there are some big differences _____ _____ _____. First of all… their bodies. River otters have narrower faces than sea otters. Also, a sea otter's rear paws _____ _____ _____ a paddle, but a river otter's have webbed toes. Oh… and one more — river otters have longer tails.

But what if you can't see their faces, paws, or… tails? You might still be able to, um, identify an otter… _____ _____ _____. You see, sea otters _____ _____ _____ _____ _____ in the water, and they like to float around on their backs. River otters, though, come onto land all the time… especially to eat. And when they swim, they _____ _____ _____ _____ a lot. And lastly… there's group size. Sea otters like to _____ _____ _____ _____, while, uh, river otters live in small family units. On the other hand, female river otters _____ _____ _____ three or four pups at once, but female sea otters… they have only one at a time.

VOCABULARY REVIEW

A Choose the correct word for each definition.

narrow	eternity	habitat	review	salinity	overlook

1. the area where a species lives: _____
2. an endless period of time: _____
3. to look over again: _____
4. thin; not wide: _____
5. the amount of salt in water: _____

B Choose the best word to explain the underlined word.

1. If you use the <u>rear</u> entrance, you go in the _____.
   - Ⓐ front
   - Ⓑ back
   - Ⓒ unit
   - Ⓓ body

2. If something is <u>complicated</u>, it is _____.
   - Ⓐ standard
   - Ⓑ effective
   - Ⓒ religious
   - Ⓓ complex

3. If you have an <u>influence</u> over something, you _____ it.
   - Ⓐ connect
   - Ⓑ affect
   - Ⓒ complain
   - Ⓓ quit

C Choose the best word to complete each sentence. Change the form if necessary.

left-handed	normal	offer	discovery	cube

1. He was looking for a(n) _____ guitar because he can't play a regular one.
2. The _____ of oil on their land made them rich.
3. A(n) _____ is an object with six equal sides.
4. I _____ to help, but she said she wanted to work alone.

D   **Choose the best phrase to complete each sentence.**

1. It is difficult to _____ because they look alike.
    Ⓐ keep in mind   Ⓑ break down   Ⓒ tell them apart Ⓓ make a difference

2. Some people buy blue or pink baby clothes, _____ the sex of their child.
    Ⓐ such as   Ⓑ affecting on   Ⓒ despite   Ⓓ depending on

3. Don't worry about it. It is _____ a small problem.
    Ⓐ other than   Ⓑ better than
    Ⓒ nothing more than   Ⓓ rather than

E   **Choose the word or phrase that is closest in meaning to the underlined word.**

1. She always had a strong <u>desire</u> to see Rome, Italy.
    Ⓐ principle   Ⓑ term   Ⓒ nutrient   Ⓓ wish

2. I <u>would rather</u> ride a bike than drive a car to work.
    Ⓐ decide to   Ⓑ appeal to   Ⓒ dislike to   Ⓓ prefer to

3. The government decided to <u>lower</u> tax rates.
    Ⓐ measure   Ⓑ decrease   Ⓒ equal   Ⓓ identify

4. He was supposed to share his snack, but he ate the <u>whole</u> thing.
    Ⓐ entire   Ⓑ available   Ⓒ present   Ⓓ webbed

F   **Choose the word that is the opposite of the underlined word.**

1. We were planning to go to the park, but <u>unfortunately</u> it rained.
    Ⓐ impressively   Ⓑ luckily   Ⓒ normally   Ⓓ traditionally

2. When he climbed onto the boat, his shoe fell in the water and <u>floated</u> away.
    Ⓐ blurred   Ⓑ sank   Ⓒ left   Ⓓ varied

UNIT 02

Detail

Detail questions ask about important details from the conversation or lecture.

QUESTION TYPES

1. Question forms that require one correct answer

    · According to the professor, what is the problem with the X method?
    · Which of the following is NOT mentioned about X?

2. Question forms that require two or more correct answers

    · What are the key features of X mentioned in the lecture? Click on 2 answers.
    · According to the professor, what are the reasons for X? Click on 2 answers.

BASIC DRILLS 01

1-1   Which of the following is NOT mentioned about red blood cells?

Ⓐ How long they live

Ⓑ What they do

Ⓒ How big they are

Ⓓ What they look like

1-2   Write T for True or F for False based on the lecture.

(1) The human body creates new red blood cells every day. _____

(2) Red blood cells produce oxygen that our body needs. _____

2-1   In the experiment, what caused the different impressions of Person A and Person B?

Ⓐ The tone of voice used when they were described

Ⓑ Whether or not strong words were used to describe them

Ⓒ Hidden pictures that showed each person's facial expression

Ⓓ The order in which descriptive words were presented

2-2   According to the experiment, which statement is likely to give a better impression?

Ⓐ Jack is lazy, strong, and kind.

Ⓑ Gary is kind, strong, and lazy.

Listen and fill in the blanks.

1.

Professor: There are, um, _____ _____ _____ blood cells: red blood cells, white blood cells, and platelets. Today we're, ahem, going to study red blood cells. First, their shape... uh, _____ _____ _____ _____ flattened disks. And their main job _____ _____ _____ _____ to our bodies. How? Red blood cells pick up oxygen in the lungs and distribute it to the tissues _____ _____ _____ _____ through the body. Another thing we need to know is _____ _____ _____. Each red blood cell lives _____ _____ _____ _____. So, um, every day the body produces new cells _____ _____ the ones that die.

2.

Professor: You probably know that _____ _____ are very important. It's true not only when you meet a person but also _____ _____ _____ _____ a person. In an experiment, a group of people heard a series of words _____ _____ _____ _____. Then they were supposed to decide whether that person was _____ _____ _____. First, they were told that Person A is smart, diligent, and stubborn. After that, they heard that Person B is stubborn, diligent, and smart. In fact, the words used to describe Person A and Person B were the same _____ _____ _____ _____ in which they were given. But the result was surprising. Most people _____ _____ _____ _____ _____ Person A than Person B.

BASIC DRILLS 02

1-1

Which of the following is NOT mentioned about Mars?

Ⓐ It has four seasons like Earth's.

Ⓑ Its seasons are shorter than Earth's.

Ⓒ The length of a day on Mars is similar to that on Earth.

Ⓓ The temperature on Mars is colder than that on Earth.

1-2

Choose the sentence that is closest in meaning to what you hear. 🎧

Ⓐ There is another planet that is more similar to Mars than Earth.

Ⓑ There aren't any other planets that are more similar to Mars than Earth.

2-1

Which of the following is mentioned about flamenco?

Click on 2 answers.

Ⓐ Flamenco originated from Spanish folk music.

Ⓑ Light-hearted flamenco songs usually have fast beats.

Ⓒ Flamenco is an art comprised of three different genres.

Ⓓ The most emotional styles have the most complex rhythms.

2-2

What is the lecture mainly about? 🎧

Ⓐ The three essential parts of modern flamenco

Ⓑ The patterns of rhythm and lyrics in flamenco songs

Listen and fill in the blanks.

1.

Professor: Mars resembles Earth more than it _____ _____ _____ _____. Like Earth, Mars has four seasons: spring, summer, fall, and winter. But, um, the seasons on Mars are longer. Another thing: _____ _____ is 24 hours and 39 minutes on Mars, which is — ahem — _____ _____ _____ Earth's 24-hour days. What was the other thing I wanted to mention? Oh yes, its temperature. Mars' temperature _____ _____ _____ Earth's. Although Mars is much colder, with a range from about –113 °C to 20 °C, its temperature is _____ _____ _____ Earth's than any of the other planets.

2.

Professor: Flamenco is a passionate, deeply emotional _____ _____ _____ _____ singing, guitar playing, and dancing. _____ _____ _____ flamenco is the song. Flamenco songs fall into three categories: profound songs, intermediate songs, light songs. Each has _____ _____ _____ rhythm and lyrics. The profound song, or deep song, _____ _____ a complex 12-beat rhythm, is the oldest form. It deals with _____ _____. Common themes include death, sorrow, despair, and anger. The intermediate song is less complex and incorporates other Spanish music styles. It is more lively and _____ _____ _____ by guitars, castanets, and hand clapping. The light song is the simplest of the three styles. It has a quick, light rhythm and deals with lighter themes such as love and humor.

LISTENING PRACTICE 01

LIBRARY

📋 **NOTE-TAKING**

Overdue fine

- _____ _____ late
- Late fee: 25 cents a day _____ _____ / in total $21

Reservation

- All the copies _____ _____
- The earliest copy due back in _____ _____

Interlibrary Services

- Receive an email when the book _____ _____ for pickup
- Register for _____ _____ to pick it up

1   Why is the student visiting the library?
   (A) To reserve a newly arrived book
   (B) To pick up a requested book
   (C) To check out a book for research
   (D) To inquire about an overdue notice

2   What does the librarian suggest?
   (A) Copying a portion of the book
   (B) Making a reservation for the book
   (C) Requesting the purchase of the book
   (D) Borrowing the book from another library

Listen and fill in the blanks.

Student: Hi. I have _____ _____ _____ _____. Unfortunately, they're late.

Librarian: Okay. Let me take a look at them.

S: Here you go.

L: These are all two weeks late. The fee is 25 cents per day. And that's for each late book. So your late fees _____ _____ $21.

S: All right. *[Pause]* Could you also _____ _____ _____ something else? I was looking for a book, but I couldn't find it. Could you check if you have it? Here's the title and author.

L: Let's see. *[Pause]* Sorry. All our copies _____ _____ _____ _____.

S: That's too bad. Is it possible _____ _____ _____ _____?

L: Sure. Just give me your name and email address. We'll notify you when _____ _____ _____ _____.

S: Thanks, I appreciate it. When do you think that will be?

L: Let's have a look… The earliest copy _____ _____ _____ in three weeks.

S: Three weeks? That's too long! I need it _____ _____ _____.

L: Well, you can try Interlibrary Services on our website. You should be able to get it from another library sooner.

S: That's great. I haven't used that service before. I _____ _____ _____ that book right away.

L: If you do, you'll _____ _____ _____ by email when the book is available for pickup. There will also be a link to a page where you can _____ _____ _____ to pick it up.

S: Thank you so much.

LISTENING PRACTICE 02

PHYSICS

📋 NOTE-TAKING

Thermometer

; thermo → _____, meter → _____

Liquids change _____ (cold → ↓, warm → ↑)

Q. liquid = _____?

A. No, _____ below _____

   → _____ : not freezing, sensitive to _____ _____

1   **What does the professor mainly discuss?**

    Ⓐ Ways of measuring temperature

    Ⓑ Special uses of thermometers

    Ⓒ How a thermometer works

    Ⓓ Different types of thermometers

2   **What does the professor say about mercury?**

    Click on 2 answers.

    Ⓐ It was the liquid used in early thermometers.

    Ⓑ It is affected by the slightest changes in temperature.

    Ⓒ It takes up less space as the temperature rises.

    Ⓓ It can measure temperatures below the freezing point.

Listen and fill in the blanks.

Professor: A thermometer is a tool that _____ _____ _____ of things. Its

name _____ _____ _____ _____ two smaller words: "thermo,"

meaning heat, and "meter," meaning to measure.

The basic principle behind thermometers is that liquids _____ _____

_____ _____ with changes in their temperature. At cold temperatures,

their volume will decrease. _____ _____ _____ _____,

their volume will increase. These changes are small, so you _____

_____ _____ in something such as... say a glass of milk. But the liquid

in thermometers _____ _____ _____ a very thin tube, which makes

these changes much _____ _____ _____.

Student: So, what kind of liquid is used in thermometers? Is it water?

P: Early thermometers used water. But water _____ _____ _____ and

that's a big problem, isn't it? Instead, mercury _____ _____ _____,

which, um, solves the freezing problem. In addition, it is sensitive to changes in

temperature, and _____ _____ _____ with these changes. Therefore,

the slightest change in temperature is easily measured with a thermometer.

LISTENING **PRACTICE 03**

PHILOSOPHY

📋 **NOTE-TAKING**

Prisoner's Dilemma

Situation: criminal A, B

① If A & B don't confess → _____ sentences

② If A & B confess → _____ sentences

③ If A confesses & B doesn't → A: free, B: _____ sentences

⇨ A & B don't _____ each other & concerned with own interests

∴ _____ _____ & get _____ sentences

---

1   What is the lecture mainly about?

ⓐ Ways to make prisoners confess

ⓑ Difficulties in decision making

ⓒ The purpose of classic game theory

ⓓ Principles of the prisoner's dilemma

2   Why are both prisoners likely to get 5-year sentences?

Click on 2 answers.

ⓐ Because they won't confess their crime

ⓑ Because they only care about their own interests

ⓒ Because they have told a lie about their crime

ⓓ Because they aren't sure whether their partner confessed

Listen and fill in the blanks.

Professor: The prisoner's dilemma is a classic example of game theory, which explains

_____-_____ _____. In the prisoner's dilemma, two criminals, A and

B, are put into two cells after they _____ _____ _____ together. The

police know they committed the crime but still _____ _____ _____.

So they tell criminal A this — if neither A nor B confesses to the crime, they'll both

get 1-year sentences. If _____ _____ _____ confess, they'll get

5-year sentences. However, if A confesses while B doesn't confess, A _____

_____ _____ _____ and B will get a 10-year sentence. The police

tell criminal B _____ _____ _____.

Student: The best case scenario is... um, _____ _____ _____

_____ and both get 1-year sentences.

P: Yes. If A and B trust each other, they can _____ _____ _____.

But _____ _____ _____ _____ the other will confess or not.

Besides, each wants to walk free and is only concerned with _____ _____

_____. As a result, they both confess and get 5-year sentences! That's the

prisoner's dilemma. It shows that... without trust, well, each person will think only

of themselves, which can lead to _____ _____ _____ _____

_____.

iBT PRACTICE

TOEFL Listening

VOLUME   HELP   OK   NEXT

OFFICE HOURS

📋 NOTE-TAKING

Go to _____ _____ or find a job?

• Go to _____ _____

• Not sure about _____ _____

Pros and cons of dual degree programs

• Ask herself whether or not to pursue a dual degree

_____ _____ _____ _____ to discuss MBA programs

1. What problem does the student have?

   Ⓐ She can't pay for graduate school.

   Ⓑ She needs to improve her communication skills.

   Ⓒ She can't choose a graduate program to apply to.

   Ⓓ She isn't sure about possible jobs after graduation.

2. What does the professor suggest?

   Ⓐ Contacting admissions officers

   Ⓑ Meeting to discuss possibilities

   Ⓒ Working while taking an MBA course

   Ⓓ Researching career paths in business

3. According to the professor, what are the key points when considering a dual degree?
   Click on 2 answers.

   Ⓐ Having a clear plan for her future

   Ⓑ Getting financial help from her parents

   Ⓒ Being equally interested in both fields

   Ⓓ Being okay with spending extra years in school

4. What does the professor imply when he says this: 🎧

   Ⓐ He is not sure the fields are right for her.

   Ⓑ He thinks the student should decide on a field.

   Ⓒ He is sure earning two degrees at once is rewarding.

   Ⓓ He wants the student to figure out if a dual degree is the best option.

Listen and fill in the blanks.

Student: Hi, Dr. Connelly. Do you have a minute?

Professor: Certainly, Anna. Why don't you sit down?

S: Well, I need your advice. You know that next semester is my last one. Then I'll graduate, and I'm not sure what to do.

P: Ah, yes. Well, that is a big step, and there are a lot of options to consider. I suppose you're already _____ _____ _____ as your field.

S: Yes, I love this field.

P: Then, mainly, you have to decide if you're going to _____ _____ _____ _____ or go to graduate school. Have you thought about that?

S: I have, and I think I want to _____ _____ _____ _____. But I am also interested in communication programs. I believe strategic communication skills are _____ _____ _____ _____ in business.

P: I couldn't agree with you more. Um ... Some schools offer dual degree programs. You might find one that offers both MBA and communication degrees.

S: That sounds great.

P: Hmm ... with a dual degree, you'll broaden your knowledge and _____ _____ _____ in your career path. However, you will _____ _____ _____ _____ in school. It will also require a lot of money. Above all, are you equally passionate about both fields?

S: Um ... I think I need to ask myself if a dual degree _____ _____ _____ me.

P: Well, why don't we _____ _____ _____ _____ to talk more? You could consider if you'll pursue a dual degree or not, and I'll suggest a few MBA programs.

S: That would be so helpful!

VOCABULARY REVIEW

A Choose the correct word for each definition.

notify	pursue	request	require	sentence	thermometer

1. to seek to accomplish a goal over a long period: _____
2. a tool used to measure temperature: _____
3. to need something for a particular purpose: _____
4. to inform of something in a formal manner: _____
5. a punishment given to a criminal by a judge: _____

B Choose the best word to explain the underlined word.

1. If you do an <u>experiment</u>, you _____ a theory.
   - Ⓐ grade
   - Ⓑ work
   - Ⓒ test
   - Ⓓ freeze

2. If something is <u>profound</u>, it has deep and _____ quality.
   - Ⓐ intense
   - Ⓑ important
   - Ⓒ enormous
   - Ⓓ grave

3. If you <u>incorporate</u> something, you _____ it as part of a whole.
   - Ⓐ specify
   - Ⓑ include
   - Ⓒ relate
   - Ⓓ apply

4. If you look for <u>evidence</u>, you are searching for _____.
   - Ⓐ theory
   - Ⓑ order
   - Ⓒ proof
   - Ⓓ volume

C Choose the best word or phrase to complete each sentence. Change the form if necessary.

passionate	life span	confess	resemble	freezing point

1. The killer finally _____ his crime.
2. He gave a _____ speech on human rights.
3. Some insects have a _____ of just one day.
4. The boy _____ his mother but acts like his father.

D Choose the best phrase to complete each sentence.

1. I _____ meet my friend for lunch, but I had to cancel.
   - Ⓐ didn't want to
   - Ⓑ wasn't allowed to
   - Ⓒ was supposed to
   - Ⓓ failed to

2. This sofa _____ too much room. We need a smaller one.
   - Ⓐ breaks off
   - Ⓑ takes place
   - Ⓒ takes up
   - Ⓓ gives off

3. The doctor ordered _____ tests to see what was wrong.
   - Ⓐ a series of
   - Ⓑ a bit of
   - Ⓒ the same as
   - Ⓓ the best of

E Choose the word that is closest in meaning to the underlined word.

1. This special offer is only <u>available</u> online.
   - Ⓐ visible
   - Ⓑ disposable
   - Ⓒ obtainable
   - Ⓓ usable

2. The budget needs to be divided <u>equally</u> between you.
   - Ⓐ impartially
   - Ⓑ open-mindedly
   - Ⓒ objectively
   - Ⓓ evenly

3. When you have a <u>dilemma</u>, it helps to talk it over with a friend.
   - Ⓐ impression
   - Ⓑ outcome
   - Ⓒ problem
   - Ⓓ formation

4. The outdoor furniture is long <u>overdue</u> for replacement.
   - Ⓐ unpaid
   - Ⓑ delayed
   - Ⓒ unsettled
   - Ⓓ outdated

F Choose the word that is the opposite of the underlined word.

1. This book is very <u>similar</u> to the author's previous work.
   - Ⓐ better
   - Ⓑ unlike
   - Ⓒ related
   - Ⓓ focused

2. Reading is a powerful way to <u>broaden</u> your perspectives.
   - Ⓐ specify
   - Ⓑ specialize
   - Ⓒ limit
   - Ⓓ restrict

3. The historic monument is located at a <u>strategic</u> site.
   - Ⓐ unintentional
   - Ⓑ unimportant
   - Ⓒ undeliberate
   - Ⓓ unplanned

Actual
Practice
Test

ACTUAL

PRACTICE

TEST **01**

ACTUAL

PRACTICE

TEST **02**

ACTUAL PRACTICE TEST 01

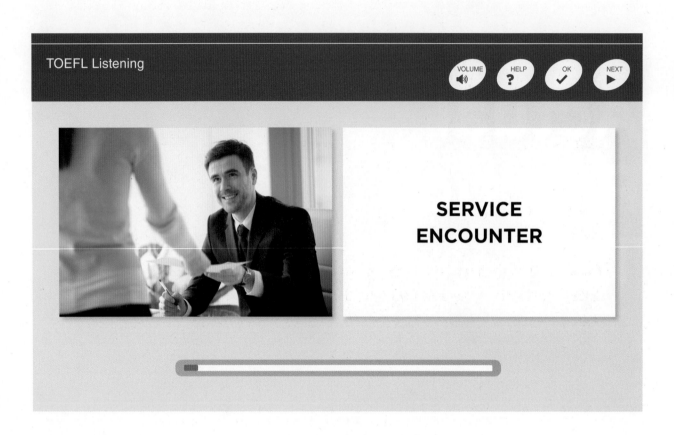

TOEFL Listening

VOLUME HELP OK NEXT

SERVICE
ENCOUNTER

📋 NOTE-TAKING

Problem: Can't get the _____ to _____

• Why did you _____ it?

Was hot because of _____ _____

Bigger problem: Radiator _____ _____! → steam & _____ water

How long will it take to _____?

→ take a while

I will _____ _____ _____ tonight

→ Okay, I'll fix it ASAP

TOEFL Listening

VOLUME HELP OK NEXT

1. Why does the student go to see the janitor?

  Ⓐ To thank him for fixing her window

  Ⓑ To complain that her room is too hot

  Ⓒ To tell him that her radiator is broken

  Ⓓ To inform him that she is moving out

2. Why does the janitor mention what month it is?

  Ⓐ To explain why he was away on vacation last week

  Ⓑ To question why she would want to open her window

  Ⓒ To suggest that she shouldn't be using her radiator

  Ⓓ To emphasize how recently he last fixed her window

3. What can be inferred about the dormitory's heating system?

  Ⓐ It doesn't work properly.

  Ⓑ It was recently installed.

  Ⓒ It hasn't worked for days.

  Ⓓ It will be replaced soon.

Listen again to part of the conversation. Then answer the question.

4. What does the janitor mean when he says this: 🎧

  Ⓐ He doesn't believe what she said.

  Ⓑ He thinks the problem is serious.

  Ⓒ He doesn't feel very well.

  Ⓓ He thinks he can fix the radiator quickly.

Listen again to part of the conversation. Then answer the question.

5. What does the student imply when she says this: 🎧

  Ⓐ She doesn't think the janitor can fix the radiator.

  Ⓑ She is worried about where she will stay tonight.

  Ⓒ She wants an answer from the janitor now.

  Ⓓ She hasn't told the janitor the whole problem.

ACTUAL PRACTICE TEST 02

ART HISTORY

📋 **NOTE-TAKING**

Muybridge: father of the _____ _____

Discussion: Does a horse lift all its _____ _____ _____ _____ when it runs?

→ photographed a running horse with _____ _____

Later, worked on other projects

→ helped _____ invent _____ _____ _____

VOLUME HELP OK NEXT

PART A

ACTUAL PRACTICE TEST

6. What is the lecture mainly about?

Ⓐ Why the motion picture was not created until 1872

Ⓑ Why Eadweard Muybridge is "the father of the motion picture"

Ⓒ How scientists discovered that horses lift their legs off the ground

Ⓓ How Thomas Edison helped Eadweard Muybridge with an invention

7. Why does the professor mention the arguments about the way horses run?

Ⓐ To emphasize the main function of early motion pictures

Ⓑ To show that Muybridge wanted to be California's governor

Ⓒ To give an example of the biggest arguments in sports history

Ⓓ To explain why Muybridge decided to take a series of pictures

8. How was Muybridge's creation different from modern motion pictures?

Ⓐ It did not use more than one camera.

Ⓑ It was not displayed in public.

Ⓒ It showed an animal in motion.

Ⓓ It was a series of photographs.

Listen again to part of the lecture. Then answer the question.

9. What can be inferred about the student?

Ⓐ She does not know how Muybridge filmed the horse.

Ⓑ She thinks Edison was the one who filmed the horse.

Ⓒ She does not think Edison invented the motion picture camera.

Ⓓ She wants to know why Muybridge did not use a motion picture camera.

PART

Pragmatic Understanding Questions

Function

- Function questions ask why the speaker makes a certain statement.
- You will often be asked to listen again to part of the conversation or lecture before answering the question.

QUESTION TYPES

· Why does the man/woman say this: 🎧

· What does the professor mean when he/she says this: 🎧

· What does the man/woman imply when he/she says this: 🎧

BASIC DRILLS 01

Listen again to part of the lecture. Then answer the question.

1-1   Why does the professor say this: 🎧
   (A) To introduce a new idea
   (B) To emphasize an important point
   (C) To give the students a hint
   (D) To remind the students of the topic of the lecture

1-2   Write T for True or F for False based on the lecture.
   (1) Weight on Earth is six times greater than it is on the Moon. _____
   (2) Your mass changes depending on your weight. _____

Listen again to part of the lecture. Then answer the question.

2-1   What does the professor mean when he says this: 🎧
   (A) He wants the students to ask more questions.
   (B) He thinks it is necessary to explain with an example.
   (C) He wants the students to research the topic on their own.
   (D) He thinks he gave enough answers to the student's question.

2-2   Choose the sentence that is closest in meaning to what you hear. 🎧
   (A) More than 5,000 artists were members in 1936, and eight years later there were about 10,000.
   (B) More than 5,000 artists were members in 1936, twice as many as there had been eight years earlier.

Listen and fill in the blanks.

1.

Professor: Generally, we do not clearly distinguish _____ _____ _____.
However, they are totally different. Mass is how much matter an object contains.
It is the same _____ _____ _____. On the other hand, weight is a
measurement of how hard _____ _____ _____ at the mass. So, your
weight depends on how much gravity is _____ _____ _____ at the
moment. Here's a question. What would your weight be on the Moon? Remember
that the gravity of the Moon is _____ _____ _____ that of Earth.

Student: I would weigh _____ _____ _____ _____ on Earth, right?

P: Right. But remember that mass is always the same _____ _____
_____ _____ or on the Moon.

2.

Professor: The Federal Art Project, known as the FAP, was created during the New
Deal to _____ _____ _____ _____ during the Depression.
Participating artists were paid $23.50 a week, _____ _____ _____
they created one major work of art or _____ _____ _____ working
on a project.

Student: Did it work?

P: Well... by 1936, more than 5,000 artists had joined, and that number probably
_____ _____ _____ _____ _____ of the project.
It produced a total of more than 100,000 easel paintings, 17,000 sculptures,
_____ _____ _____ nearly 300,000 fine prints. The final cost was
more than $35,000,000. Do I _____ _____ _____ _____?

BASIC DRILLS 02

Listen again to part of the lecture. Then answer the question.

1-1 Why does the professor say this: 🎧
- (A) To offer a different opinion
- (B) To introduce another example
- (C) To correct a common misunderstanding
- (D) To remind the students of an important point

1-2 Choose the sentence that is closest in meaning to what you hear. 🎧
- (A) They can explain what is happening to them by sending out vibrations.
- (B) They can figure out what is happening near them by feeling vibrations.

Listen again to part of the lecture. Then answer the question.

2-1 Why does the professor say this: 🎧
- (A) To correct a wrong idea
- (B) To point out an important rule
- (C) To change the topic of the lecture
- (D) To summarize the lecture

2-2 According to the professor, what is important in interpreting literature?
- (A) Interpretation should be based on personal feelings and beliefs.
- (B) Interpretation should be supported with details from the text.

Listen and fill in the blanks.

1.

Professor: Spiders have poor vision, _____ _____ _____ more than darkness, light, and basic shapes, but they do have a very good _____ _____ _____. _____ _____ _____, they are able to understand what is happening around them. When their web shakes, for example, they can tell if it was caused by the wind or _____ _____ _____ they can eat. This is because insects _____ _____ _____, while the wind causes smooth vibrations. And _____ _____ _____. When a male spider visits the web of a female spider to mate, he sends her special vibrations so she knows who he is and _____ _____ _____.

2.

Professor: We've been talking about _____ _____ _____ literature, and we've found that not everybody will always read the same story the same way. It's understood that _____ _____ _____ _____ to interpret literature, and, in fact, some works are intentionally written to suggest _____ _____ _____ _____ interpretation. But... let me make something clear. Although there is no right or wrong way to read a story, your interpretation must come _____ _____ _____ _____. What I'm saying is, sometimes we use our own feelings and beliefs to create meanings that _____ _____ _____. But the interpretation of literature is like scientific theory in a way... it must be _____ _____ _____ from the text.

LISTENING PRACTICE 01

OFFICE HOURS

📝 NOTE-TAKING

Purpose: Want to submit essay to _____ _____

Major in _____?
- No, _____.

Essay was written for _____ _____?
- Yes, but I _____ it.

⇨ Okay

_____? – Bronte sisters' novels

---

1 **Why does the student visit the professor?**
- Ⓐ To talk about changing her major to philosophy
- Ⓑ To enter an essay in a writing contest
- Ⓒ To get some advice on an essay she is writing
- Ⓓ To hand in a report for her English class

Listen again to part of the conversation. Then answer the question.

2 **Why does the professor say this:** 🎧
- Ⓐ To give the reason the student needs to write a new essay
- Ⓑ To persuade the student to major in English
- Ⓒ To let the student know why he asked such questions
- Ⓓ To tell the student that she cannot apply for the contest

Listen and fill in the blanks.

Professor: Hello. Can I help you?

Student: Hello, Professor Nordstrom. Is it okay _____ _____ _____ _____ _____ to the English department's writing contest?

P: Oh, certainly. Please have a seat. *[pause]* You don't _____ _____. What's your name?

S: Marilyn Gilmore, sir.

P: Marilyn Gilmore? _____ _____ _____ _____ English?

S: No, I'm not. Actually, I've decided to major in philosophy.

P: Philosophy? Hmm... I see. Um, _____ _____ _____ _____ in a course from the English department?

S: Yes, it was _____ _____ _____ Professor Stein's Introduction to English Literature class last semester. But I've _____ _____ _____ _____ _____ since then.

P: Professor Stein's class? Okay. Well, that's fine, then. If you're not an English major and want to _____ _____ _____ _____, you need to have taken some English courses.

S: Great. Here it is.

P: Thank you. And what's the topic of your essay?

S: I wrote about the Bronte sisters, Emily and Charlotte. It's a _____ _____ their novels.

P: That's an excellent topic. I look forward to reading it.

LISTENING PRACTICE 02

BOTANY

📋 **NOTE-TAKING**

Savanna: between tropical _____ _____ and _____
- warm, rainy (only _____)
- dry _____ → water stress of plants & many _____

How plants grow: _____
① water: storing in trunks / using _____ _____ / losing leaves
② fire: keeping buds _____ & having _____ _____

1 What is the lecture mainly about?
   Ⓐ The characteristics of the savanna climate
   Ⓑ Why plant species are decreasing in the savanna
   Ⓒ The role of water and fire in the savanna
   Ⓓ How savanna plants survive in their environment

Listen again to part of the lecture. Then answer the question.

2 Why does the professor say this: 🎧
   Ⓐ To explain the difference in meaning
   Ⓑ To help the students understand
   Ⓒ To correct a mistake he made
   Ⓓ To emphasize the focus of the lecture

Listen and fill in the blanks.

Professor: The savanna is _____ _____ _____ tropical grasslands located between a tropical rain forest and a desert. It can be found mostly in the plains of Africa. The savanna _____ _____ _____ _____, and rain falls mostly during the summer. In winter, the dry season, it _____ _____ _____ and plants experience water stress. Yes, it's the kind of stress you know. Fires are also common at this time, because the dead, dry leaves burn very easily.

_____ _____ _____ _____, a variety of plants grow in the savanna. So, how do they do it? Adaptation. When there is a drought, they survive _____ _____ _____ in their trunks and reaching underground water _____ _____ _____ _____. They also save water by, um, by losing their leaves in the winter. Some plants have adapted to _____ _____ _____, as well. Their buds _____ _____ _____ underground, and many of the trees of the savanna _____ _____ by thick bark. And others, such as the baobab tree, _____ _____ _____ both fire and drought by storing water in their bark and trunk.

LISTENING **PRACTICE 03**

SPORTS

📋 **NOTE-TAKING**

Warming-up

- helps avoid _____ and should be done _____ _____

Q. stretching ≠ warming up?

A. warming up → raise _____ _____

   stretching → _____ _____ (without warming up → _____)

   e.g. _____ _____ or aerobic dance

1 What is the lecture mainly about?

Ⓐ The importance of warming up before exercise

Ⓑ Types of injuries that are caused by stretching

Ⓒ Tips on how to live a longer and healthier life

Ⓓ The effects of warming up and stretching

Listen again to part of the lecture. Then answer the question.

2 Why does the professor say this: 🎧

Ⓐ To introduce a new idea into the lecture

Ⓑ To get back to the point of the lecture

Ⓒ To agree with the student's idea

Ⓓ To correct the student's misunderstanding

Listen and fill in the blanks.

Professor: One of the most important steps in _____ _____ _____ _____ is properly warming up. Warming up _____ _____ _____ _____ by raising your body temperature, which lets your muscles know that they need to _____ _____ _____ _____. It should always be done before you start stretching... usually a mild activity such as slowly running in place is best.

Student: Excuse me. Did you say it _____ _____ _____ _____ _____? I always thought stretching was actually a warm-up activity.

P: Well, some people may call stretching a warm-up. But we warm up to _____ _____ _____ _____, and we stretch to _____ _____ _____. And you really should warm up before you stretch. Stretching without raising your body temperature could _____ _____ _____ _____ to your cold muscles. So before you exercise — and before you stretch — always warm up to get your heart pumping and your blood flowing to your muscles. Either a slow jog or a bit of aerobic dance _____ _____ _____ _____ _____ to get your body ready.

iBT PRACTICE

TOEFL Listening

VOLUME · HELP · OK · NEXT

ECONOMICS

📋 **NOTE-TAKING**

Unhealthy _____ starts:

- Rising _____ mean rising collateral values.
- Banks offer larger _____ as collateral values rise.
- People borrows more, increase the demand, drive up prices

Bubble expands:

- Banks lend money even to low-_____ borrowers
- People buy homes to get _____

Bubble pops:

- Most borrowers can't repay their _____
- Increase stops or _____ _____ → panic and a crash

1. What is the lecture mainly about?
   - Ⓐ Bubbles that led to financial crises
   - Ⓑ Debt causing bubbles to grow beyond control
   - Ⓒ Borrowing as a cause of economic collapse
   - Ⓓ Investors taking advantage of low-income borrowers

2. According to the professor, why do banks give mortgages to people with low incomes?
   - Ⓐ Banks earn money even when homes lose value.
   - Ⓑ Banks believe the economy is never going to slow down.
   - Ⓒ Banks assume that house prices will continue to grow.
   - Ⓓ Banks make more profit on high-risk mortgages than low-risk ones.

3. Which of the following is mentioned as a way debt drives bubbles?
   Click on 3 answers.
   - Ⓐ By allowing home values to drop
   - Ⓑ By forcing prices above real values
   - Ⓒ By creating an impression of low risk
   - Ⓓ By enabling low-income people to borrow
   - Ⓔ By giving high profits to banks but not to borrowers

Listen again to part of the lecture. Then answer the question.

4. Why does the professor says this: 🎧
   - Ⓐ To explain that mortgages can be risky
   - Ⓑ To suggest that banks are behaving unethically
   - Ⓒ To show that borrowers have an understandable motivation
   - Ⓓ To illustrate how debt can be used as a tool in strong economies

Listen and fill in the blanks.

Professor: Good morning, class. Today, we're talking about debt-driven bubbles in housing prices. When a home buyer borrows money, the house itself serves as collateral for the loan. Hmm … I don't think you're _____ _____ that term, collateral. It's a kind of security. If the borrower fails to repay the loan, the bank _____ _____ _____ _____ the house to pay it off.

Getting back to the point, higher house prices mean _____ _____ _____. That is, when house prices rise, the collateral values increase; and banks are more willing to lend mortgages. As loans become _____ _____ _____, more buyers take out loans, increase the demand for houses, and drive up house prices. Moreover, when house prices rapidly rise, banks _____ _____ _____. Now, they are willing to lend large amounts of money to people even _____ _____ _____ _____. Meanwhile, people start to borrow more _____ _____ _____ by reselling houses. They don't need homes and can't actually pay for them. They only want a piece of the pie, right? As long as _____ _____ _____, all houses are increasing in value; all loans are getting paid off. Both lenders and borrowers conclude the risk is low. The bubble _____ _____ _____ _____. And, sooner or later, home values stop increasing. The bubble pops.

S: Why do the home values stop increasing, though?

P: Well, there are many factors, but it's mostly because their real value was _____ _____ _____. Remember, in this situation, most borrowers can't really repay their loans. If the increase stops or even slows down, there can be a panic and a crash. As we know, the real estate bubble in the United States triggered the 2008 _____ _____ _____.

VOCABULARY REVIEW

A   Choose the correct word for each definition.

sense	import	easel	vision	bark

1. the ability to see: _____
2. a stand used to hold an artist's canvas: _____
3. the outer layer of a tree: _____
4. to buy from another country: _____

B   Choose the best word or phrase to explain the underlined word.

1. If something has a great value, it is _____.
   - Ⓐ insignificant
   - Ⓑ priceless
   - Ⓒ valueless
   - Ⓓ invalid

2. If you set standards, you establish a(n) _____ in evaluations.
   - Ⓐ criticism
   - Ⓑ instruction
   - Ⓒ measure
   - Ⓓ option

3. If you summarize something, you give a(n) _____ of it.
   - Ⓐ abstarct
   - Ⓑ contraction
   - Ⓒ interpretation
   - Ⓓ synopsis

4. If you trigger something, you get it _____.
   - Ⓐ ceased
   - Ⓑ finished
   - Ⓒ resolved
   - Ⓓ prompted

C   Choose the best word or phrase to complete each sentence. Change the form if necessary.

fine print	rain forests	plains	drought	trunk

1. We must not waste water because we're in a _____.
2. The Amazonian _____ are being cut down.
3. _____ are flat lands with few trees.
4. You can tell the age of a tree by counting the rings on its _____.

D Choose the best phrase to complete each sentence.

1. It is important to eat _____ fruits and vegetables.
   - (A) in terms of
   - (B) a kind of
   - (C) a variety of
   - (D) a part of

2. The film _____ a true story.
   - (A) is based on
   - (B) applies for
   - (C) is adapted to
   - (D) stores up

3. He has a lot of problems to _____ right now.
   - (A) take up
   - (B) deal with
   - (C) act on
   - (D) cool down

E Choose the word or phrase that is closest in meaning to the underlined word.

1. The teacher <u>emphasized</u> the importance of literature.
   - (A) corrected
   - (B) summarized
   - (C) stressed
   - (D) revised

2. I have to <u>submit</u> my paper by five o'clock today.
   - (A) hand in
   - (B) give up
   - (C) complete
   - (D) type

3. There are <u>various</u> options to choose from.
   - (A) familiar
   - (B) several
   - (C) questionable
   - (D) effective

4. The book is a useful <u>introduction</u> to British literature.
   - (A) beginning
   - (B) middle
   - (C) conclusion
   - (D) end

F Choose the word that is the opposite of the underlined word.

1. The baby's skin was soft and <u>smooth</u>.
   - (A) clear
   - (B) rough
   - (C) mild
   - (D) sweet

2. Getting married is a <u>major</u> event in one's life.
   - (A) cheap
   - (B) sad
   - (C) minor
   - (D) confusing

3. The world economy was <u>expanding</u> at a modest pace in October.
   - (A) abridging
   - (B) condensing
   - (C) contracting
   - (D) concluding

Attitude

- Attitude questions ask how the speaker feels about something in the conversation or lecture. They also ask how certain the speaker is about something in the conversation or lecture.

- You will often be asked to listen again to part of the conversation or lecture before answering the question.

QUESTION TYPES

- What is the speaker's attitude toward X?
- What is the speaker's opinion of X?
- What can be inferred about the student?
- What does the professor mean when he/she says this: 🎧

BASIC DRILLS 01

1-1 What is the professor's opinion about dams?

ⓐ She thinks they are a new energy source that can replace fossil fuels.

ⓑ She believes that they are clean and safe because they produce little pollution.

ⓒ She thinks they can have a bad influence on the environment.

ⓓ She believes they should be built where fossil fuels are not found.

1-2 What is the general opinion about dams?

ⓐ They harm the environment.

ⓑ They are clean and safe.

Listen again to part of the lecture. Then answer the question.

2-1 What can be inferred about the professor?

ⓐ He is interested in setting up a new tax system.

ⓑ He supports the idea behind the progressive tax system.

ⓒ He agrees with what the student has just said.

ⓓ He believes the progressive tax system gives rich people an advantage.

2-2 What is the progressive tax system?

ⓐ Increasing the tax rate with increasing income

ⓑ Applying the same tax rate to everyone

Listen and fill in the blanks.

1.

Professor: Dams are _____ _____ _____ _____ from flowing water. People generally have a good opinion of them. They think that unlike fossil fuels, dams don't produce large amounts of pollution that causes _____ _____. So dams _____ _____ _____ _____ a clean and environmentally safe way of producing electricity.

However, flooding large areas of land creates a lot of greenhouse gases. As _____ _____ _____ _____, they produce greenhouse gases such as carbon dioxide. In the end, the amounts produced _____ _____ _____ _____ _____ those produced by other sources of electricity. Do you understand what I'm saying? It means that dams might _____ _____ _____ _____ in global warming as well.

2.

Professor: The overall tax system in the U.S. is progressive, meaning the percentage of tax _____ _____ _____ _____ increasing income. Those _____ _____ _____ pay more in total taxes and a higher rate of taxes. For example, a person making $100,000 annually might pay 25% of their income in taxes, while someone with an income of $30,000 _____ _____ _____ _____.

Student: But... rich people might think _____ _____ _____.

P: Yes, they might. But the concept behind the progressive tax system is that _____ _____ _____ _____ should pay more because they can do so without having to give up anything important. I mean... the money _____ _____ _____ _____ wouldn't be needed to buy basic necessities.

BASIC DRILLS 02

1-1

What can be inferred about the professor?

(A) She doubts eating meat harms the environment.

(B) She believes a vegetarian diet is more ethical.

(C) She believes people should choose plant-based diets.

(D) She is sure that everyday food choices could benefit the planet.

1-2

Choose the sentence that is the closest in meaning to what you hear. 🎧

(A) Vegetarians are less concerned about environmental problems.

(B) Most vegetarians don't realize that their diets can help the environment.

2-1

What is the professor's opinion about the Barbizon painters?

(A) They developed a new style of landscape painting.

(B) They were impressed by classical landscape painting.

(C) They went against tradition but failed to change it.

(D) Their style was superior to classical painting.

2-2

Choose the sentence that is closest in meaning to what you hear. 🎧

(A) Unlike classical painters, they removed background landscapes and focused on the painting's main subject.

(B) Unlike classical painters, their style made landscapes the focus of the painting, not just the background.

Listen and fill in the blanks.

1.

Professor: According to a study, most people _____ _____ _____ vegetarian because they care about animal welfare or because they want to be healthier. Few do so _____ _____ _____ for the environment. As it shows, people _____ _____ _____ of the impact eating meat has on the environment. However, what we eat matters environmentally. Researchers examined 300 _____ _____ _____. They found the food _____ _____ _____ _____ was beef. When they replaced beef with chicken, it dramatically reduced the average carbon footprints of the diets by 54%. In addition, the revised diets _____ _____ _____ in their Healthy Eating Index scores. Lower-carbon diets can be healthier, too. Practically speaking, eating no meat may not be the best idea, but eating less meat will _____ _____ _____.

2.

Professor: The Barbizon school was a group of 19th century French _____ _____. Instead of classical paintings in which the landscape was _____ _____ _____ the background, they created paintings _____ _____ _____ the beauty of the landscape itself. The Barbizon painters each _____ _____ _____ _____ and ideas, but they all used nature as the main subject of their paintings. And they painted _____ _____ _____ _____, rather than dramatic ones. These paintings _____ _____ _____ like the changing seasons or the changing light of the day. It was an informal school, but it played an important role in _____ _____ _____ _____ _____ landscape painting as a genre.

LISTENING PRACTICE 01

OFFICE HOURS

📋 **NOTE-TAKING**

How to write a _____ _____?

→ write your _____

not _____?

⇨ _____ + _____

there is no _____ or _____ answer

1   What is the conversation mainly about?

Ⓐ Why the student received a poor grade on a report

Ⓑ The student's fear of making mistakes in a report

Ⓒ How to write a certain kind of report

Ⓓ The professor's late homework policy

Listen again to part of the conversation. Then answer the question.

2   What can be inferred about the student?

Ⓐ He is sure that the professor made a mistake.

Ⓑ He is surprised at the professor's suggestion.

Ⓒ He is disappointed at the change in his homework assignment.

Ⓓ He is confused about the report.

Listen and fill in the blanks.

Student: Excuse me, Professor Kane. _____ _____ _____ _____ I ask you a quick question?

Professor: Of course, Shaun. Come on in.

S: Thanks. There's something I didn't really understand in class today. Um, could you please explain exactly _____ _____ _____ _____ a reaction report? I'm not sure what I'm supposed to write.

P: It's _____ _____, really. You just need to _____ _____ _____.

S: My opinion? But in class you said that it was _____ _____ _____ _____.

P: Well, yes. A reaction report should _____ _____ _____ of the material. But the most important part is _____ _____ _____ _____ interpret it.

S: How should I get started?

P: I'd suggest _____ _____ the summary. After that, you can write your personal interpretation of the material.

S: Got it. I guess I'll _____ _____ _____ _____.

P: Great. And relax, Shaun. There's no _____ _____ _____ _____ when you're writing a reaction report. Just tell me what you think _____ _____ _____.

S: All right, I will. Thanks for your help, Professor Kane.

LISTENING PRACTICE 02

HISTORY OF SCIENCE

📋 **NOTE-TAKING**

The _____ of the telescope

1. Who was the inventor? – _____? No. → used it in _____ first

               – Lippershey. Yes → _____ improved it

2. Galileo's achievements (with _____)

① _____ the stars

② proved "the _____ moves round the _____."

⇨ people believe he _____ _____

1   **What is the lecture mainly about?**

       Ⓐ Who invented the first telescope

       Ⓑ Galileo's achievements with his telescope

       Ⓒ Why Galileo's telescope was important

       Ⓓ The use of the telescope in astronomy

2   **What is the professor's opinion about the first telescope?**

       Ⓐ She thinks it was not welcomed among scientists at first.

       Ⓑ She thinks it would have been impossible without Galileo.

       Ⓒ She thinks it is still questionable who invented it.

       Ⓓ She thinks it's natural to mistake Galileo as the inventor.

Listen and fill in the blanks.

Professor: The invention of the telescope _____ _____ _____ _____ in astronomy. So, do you know who invented it? Galileo Galilei? Actually, Galileo wasn't _____ _____ _____ the telescope. He, um... he just introduced and, uh, used it in astronomy _____ _____ _____ _____.

The actual inventor of the first telescope was a Dutch eyeglass maker named Hans Lippershey, who _____ _____ _____ _____ lenses in 1608. Galileo learned of this invention in 1609. Despite _____ _____ _____ _____, he worked out the mathematics of the device and immediately _____ _____ _____ _____. With this new tool, he could _____ _____ _____ and made many great discoveries. Observations of mountains on the Moon, stars in the Milky Way, and the moons of Jupiter... these are _____ _____ his, um, major achievements. And, importantly, the use of the telescope _____ _____ _____ _____ _____ of the Copernican theory that "the Sun does not go round the Earth but the Earth rounds the Sun." He really did many great things... and made the telescope famous. So _____ _____ _____ that many people believe that he is the inventor of the telescope.

LISTENING **PRACTICE 03**

BIOLOGY

📋 **NOTE-TAKING**

Color-blindness

: not blind to _____ _____, but to certain colors

Cause

cones in the _____ (red, blue, green cones)

If not working or _____

➪ can't _____ certain colors

1   What does the professor say about color-blindness?

Ⓐ There are a lot of ways to cure it.

Ⓑ Color-blind people have trouble watching black-and-white movies.

Ⓒ Color-blind people still can see certain colors.

Ⓓ Nobody knows exactly what causes it.

Listen again to part of the lecture. Then answer the question.

2   What can be inferred about the student?

Ⓐ She is surprised at what the professor said.

Ⓑ She doubts the information given in the lecture.

Ⓒ She is sure the professor made a mistake.

Ⓓ She thinks the professor is making a joke.

Listen and fill in the blanks.

Professor: As you probably know, some people are color-blind. But this doesn't mean that they can't _____ _____ _____ _____ _____. It's not as if they're always watching a black-and-white movie. Actually, _____ _____ _____ _____ _____ to all colors. Rather, color-blind people have trouble seeing _____ _____ _____, um... between certain colors. To understand _____ _____ color-blindness, you need to know about the cones in your eyes.

Student: *[surprised]* There are cones _____ _____ _____?

P: Yes, there are, but they're very small. They're actually a type of cell _____ _____ _____ _____ _____ your eye on your retina. Different cones are _____ _____ different colors. You need three types of cones to properly see colors: red cones, blue cones, and green cones. If any of these cones _____ _____ _____ or are missing, your brain won't be able _____ _____ a certain color from another. For example, a green leaf _____ _____ _____, or a blue car might look silver. But you would still be able to see the _____ _____ _____ other colors.

iBT PRACTICE

TOEFL Listening
VOLUME   HELP   OK   NEXT

BIOLOGY

📋 **NOTE-TAKING**

Symbiosis

: _____ _____ between different organisms

Types of symbiosis

① both _____ (e.g., _____ and acacia plants)

② one _____, the other isn't _____ (e.g., orchids and tree)

③ one _____, the other is _____ (e.g., _____ and _____)

1. What is the lecture mainly about?
   (A) How symbiosis affects the balance of nature
   (B) Animals that benefit from relationships with plants
   (C) Ways that plants and animals help each other survive
   (D) Types of close relationships between two species

2. How is the lecture organized?
   (A) Various forms of symbiosis are listed with examples.
   (B) How the plants and animals help each other is described.
   (C) The importance of each type of symbiosis is compared.
   (D) How a relationship between species affects an ecosystem is explained.

3. What does the professor say about orchids?
   (A) They harm trees in order to survive.
   (B) They do not need help from another species.
   (C) They use the same kind of symbiosis as fleas.
   (D) They benefit from another organism.

Listen again to part of the lecture. Then answer the question.

4. What does the professor imply when he says this: ∩
   (A) He feels the topic is boring.
   (B) He thinks the answer is obvious.
   (C) He doesn't want to discuss the topic anymore.
   (D) He believes that no one can answer his question.

Listen and fill in the blanks.

Professor: Sometimes in nature you find two organisms that _____ _____ _____ _____. One organism — or both — needs the other to, uh, to survive. This is called symbiosis. Um, the word symbiosis basically means " _____ _____ ."

There are a few different forms of symbiosis. The first type of symbiosis involves two species that _____ _____ _____ their close relationship. Here's an example: Have you ever seen an acacia plant _____ _____ _____?

The ants get sugar and stems to live in... and acacia plants _____ _____ because the ants _____ _____ _____ _____ attackers.

See how this kind of symbiosis works? Both the ants and acacia plants are, um, _____ _____ _____ _____.

The next kind of symbiosis is similar, but instead of _____ _____ _____, only one species does. The other isn't _____ _____ _____. Orchids are an example of this kind of symbiosis. See, in rain forest, orchids grow on other plants, usually on the branches of tall trees. Orchids benefit by being on tall trees because they get _____ _____ _____ _____.

Plus, their seeds _____ _____ when they fall from way up high. The trees don't _____ _____ _____ _____ the symbiosis, but they aren't harmed, either.

The last type of symbiosis is where one species benefits and the other _____ _____. _____ _____ _____ _____ a flea on a cat. The flea is happy because it gets to feed on the cat's blood. And... how about the cat? Is the cat happy, too? This relationship is... good for the fleas but _____ _____ the cats.

VOCABULARY REVIEW

A Choose the correct word for each definition.

convince	income	impact	correctness	concern	organism

1. the amount of money that you earn: _____
2. something that is living: _____
3. to persuade someone to believe something: _____
4. the effect or influence of something on another: _____
5. the state of being right: _____

B Choose the best word or phrase to explain the underlined word.

1. If a box <u>contains</u> something, it _____ something in it.
   Ⓐ remains　　Ⓑ bounces　　Ⓒ holds　　Ⓓ reflects

2. If you do something <u>annually</u>, you do it _____.
   Ⓐ every day　　Ⓑ every year　　Ⓒ immediately　　Ⓓ forever

3. If you <u>combine</u> two things, you _____ them.
   Ⓐ defend　　Ⓑ remove　　Ⓒ fix　　Ⓓ mix

C Choose the best word to complete each sentence. Change the form if necessary.

moon	doubt	ecosystem	decay	background

1. Introducing a new animal to a region can cause problems in the _____.
2. Mars has two _____ while the Earth has one.
3. Too much sugar will cause your teeth to _____.
4. That may be true, but I _____ it.

D Choose the best phrase to complete each sentence.

1. They decided to _____ a new company.
   Ⓐ bring about   Ⓑ break down   Ⓒ set up   Ⓓ take in

2. I've never done this before, but I guess I'll _____.
   Ⓐ give it a try   Ⓑ give you back
   Ⓒ do it again   Ⓓ have it all

3. Bach _____ the father of classical music.
   Ⓐ is famous for   Ⓑ has a chance of
   Ⓒ is known as   Ⓓ has to do with

E Choose the word that is closest in meaning to the underlined word.

1. The teacher explained the new <u>concept</u> to the students.
   Ⓐ image   Ⓑ experiment   Ⓒ novel   Ⓓ idea

2. She said that finishing college was her greatest <u>achievement</u>.
   Ⓐ relationship   Ⓑ accomplishment
   Ⓒ observation   Ⓓ device

3. The answer is <u>obvious</u>.
   Ⓐ clear   Ⓑ actual   Ⓒ confusing   Ⓓ unfair

F Choose the word that is the opposite of the underlined word.

1. He wore an <u>ordinary</u> business suit.
   Ⓐ special   Ⓑ cheap   Ⓒ classical   Ⓓ dramatic

2. We hope to have made a <u>slight</u> positive contribution to the community.
   Ⓐ limitless   Ⓑ dramatic   Ⓒ extensive   Ⓓ enormous

3. The girls organized an <u>informal</u> soccer league.
   Ⓐ progressive   Ⓑ casual   Ⓒ official   Ⓓ overall

Actual
Practice
Test

ACTUAL

PRACTICE

TEST **01**

ACTUAL

PRACTICE

TEST **02**

OFFICE HOURS

📋 **NOTE-TAKING**

About the _____ magazine

Be my _____

- But I'm _____

Need _____ advice so I don't fail again

- Okay. Choose the _____?

Not chosen yet → Do not use _____ _____

⇨ Bring _____ _____ next week

TOEFL Listening

VOLUME HELP OK NEXT

1. Why does the student visit the professor?
   - (A) To see if she'll be an adviser for his magazine
   - (B) To learn more about the book she is writing
   - (C) To thank her for her help with his last magazine
   - (D) To find out why his magazine didn't win any awards

2. Why does the professor hesitate to accept the student's request?
   - (A) She thinks his ideas aren't very good.
   - (B) She doesn't think she is qualified.
   - (C) She is worried about breaking school policy.
   - (D) She feels she doesn't have enough time.

3. Why didn't the student's magazine win any awards last year?
   - (A) His classmates didn't help him out.
   - (B) Its title wasn't interesting enough.
   - (C) He failed to get professional advice.
   - (D) The university refused to publish it.

4. What is the professor's final attitude toward the student's request?
   - (A) She is still undecided.
   - (B) She has been persuaded.
   - (C) She is very excited.
   - (D) She has become annoyed.

Listen again to part of the conversation. Then answer the question.

5. Why does the professor say this: 🎧
   - (A) To agree with the student's opinion about using the university's name
   - (B) To explain why the student's idea isn't unique
   - (C) To suggest some possible names for the student's literary magazine
   - (D) To tell the student to change the title of his literary magazine

ACTUAL PRACTICE TEST 02

PHILOSOPHY

📋 **NOTE-TAKING**

Life without _____

= the _____ _____ _____

Hobbes – negative view like "_____"

_____ against everyone

How to avoid?

• Setting rules called "_____ _____"

• Everyone agrees to _____ it

VOLUME HELP OK NEXT

6. What does the professor mainly discuss?

    Ⓐ Philosophers' theories about the state of nature

    Ⓑ Hobbes' state of nature and social contract theories

    Ⓒ Why Hobbes believed it is necessary to have a social contract

    Ⓓ How human beings might live if there were no rules or laws

7. How does the professor introduce his description of the state of nature?

    Ⓐ By asking what the students would do in a certain situation

    Ⓑ By explaining the time period during which Hobbes lived

    Ⓒ By giving an example of how war causes societies to change

    Ⓓ By comparing it with other philosophers' theories

8. According to the professor, what is the purpose of a social contract?

    Ⓐ To punish people who cause troubles

    Ⓑ To maintain peace in a society

    Ⓒ To create a state of nature

    Ⓓ To improve economic conditions

Listen again to part of the lecture. Then answer the question.

9. Why does the professor say this: 🎧

    Ⓐ To introduce Hobbes' social contract theory

    Ⓑ To emphasize the weakness of Hobbes' idea

    Ⓒ To make clear the point of the state of nature theories

    Ⓓ To explain why Hobbes' theory is important

PART

Connecting Information Questions

05

Organization

- Organization questions ask about how the professor uses key details to support the main idea.
- You need to identify why the professor mentions certain things in certain places and how the professor expresses important points.

QUESTION TYPES

1. Question forms that ask about the overall organization of the lecture
   - How is the lecture organized?
   - In what order does the professor explain the topic?

2. Question forms that ask about the relationship between a specific piece of information and the lecture as a whole
   - Why does the professor mention X?

BASIC DRILLS 01

1-1   How does the professor explain the meaning of a word?
Ⓐ By comparing its two elements
Ⓑ By showing how to use a dictionary
Ⓒ By giving various examples
Ⓓ By describing how it changes over time

1-2   Indicate whether each of the following is a denotation or a connotation of "doves."
(1) peace: _____
(2) a kind of bird: _____

2-1   Why does the professor mention a bowling ball?
Ⓐ To explain how large masses curve space
Ⓑ To show how a moon orbits around its planet
Ⓒ To explain why an object falls toward the Earth
Ⓓ To demonstrate how black holes are discovered

2-2   Write T for true or F for False based on the lecture.
(1) Newton theorized why two objects are pulled together. _____
(2) Some mass doesn't pull things toward itself. _____

Listen and fill in the blanks.

1.

Professor: A word, any word, has a meaning. That's _____ _____ _____ what the word expresses. But the meaning of every word _____ _____ _____ _____. First, there is its "denotation." This is the meaning that you can _____ _____ _____ _____. Second, there is the word's "connotation." This goes _____ _____ _____ _____ _____. For example, you can find the meaning of the word "home" in the dictionary. That is the word's denotation. The connotation, however, is different. _____ _____ _____ _____ when you think of "home?"

Student: I think of warmth and love.

P: Very good. Warmth and love are _____ _____ the connotation of the word "home."

2.

Professor: Newton's law of gravity is still used, but it doesn't explain _____ _____ _____. In 1915, Einstein offered a new theory of gravity. He showed that gravity is a result of the curving of space rather than _____ _____ _____.

I'll give you an analogy. Imagine a bowling ball _____ _____ on a trampoline. The surface of the trampoline would _____ _____ instead of being flat. Now, _____ _____ a lighter ball at the edge of the trampoline. What will happen? It will roll down toward the bowling ball. This attraction to the bowling ball occurs because the trampoline curves downward, not because the two balls are actually _____ _____ _____ _____ by an invisible force. That's the way gravity works. Mass creates a depression in space, so it pulls everything toward itself. _____ _____ the mass, the harder it pulls.

BASIC DRILLS 02

1-1 Why does the professor mention stress levels?

    (A) To discuss possible results of epigenetics

    (B) To give an example of an epigenetic factor

    (C) To imply that stress changes people's DNA

    (D) To show that genes determine stress levels

1-2 Choose the sentence that is the closest in meaning to what you hear.

    (A) Certain factors may cause different parts of DNA to be used.

    (B) A variety of causes can lead to changes in DNA.

2-1 How does the professor explain papyrus paper making?

    (A) By describing the most important step in detail

    (B) By comparing it to other paper production

    (C) By introducing its process step by step

    (D) By giving an example of different usages of papyrus

2-2 Choose the sentence that is closest in meaning to what you hear.

    (A) The papyrus couldn't be used as paper until it had been dried and polished with a stone.

    (B) When the papyrus was ready to be used as paper, it would be polished with a dry stone.

Listen and fill in the blanks.

1.

Professor: Humans have about 200 types of cells. All of these cells contain approximately 20,000 identical genes. Genes are _____ _____ _____ DNA that code for proteins. However, each cell type has _____ _____ _____ _____ chemicals that determines which genes get used. These chemicals attach to the genes and turn them "on" or "off." As a result, the genes _____ _____ _____, which creates different types of cells. These "epigenetic changes" do not change the DNA sequence; instead, they affect _____ _____ _____ the genes. In fact, everything around us _____ _____ _____ that affect gene expression, including diet, age, and stress levels. This explains why _____ _____ twins can exhibit different behaviors, skills, health, and achievement. However, epigenetic changes are not permanent. Our appearance, health, and personality can all change _____ _____ _____ our surroundings.

2.

Professor: Thousands of years ago, ancient Egyptians _____ _____ _____ using the papyrus plant. They would gather this plant, which grew along the Nile River, and remove _____ _____ _____ _____ the stem. Then they would cut the rest of the stem into long, thin pieces and put it in water for several days _____ _____ _____ _____. The next step was to lay these pieces on top of one another. And this would allow the remaining sugar _____ _____ _____ _____ like glue. Another layer would _____ _____ _____ _____, and then the two layers were pounded until they stuck together. After the papyrus was allowed to dry and polished with a rock, it was _____ _____ _____ _____ as paper.

LISTENING PRACTICE 01

BIOLOGY

📋 NOTE-TAKING

The endocrine system

• _____ system in body

• Produce _____ & regulate body

Q. _____ system for communication?

A. Both are for _____ but work differently

   • Nervous system ≒ _____ : one to _____

   • Endocrine system ≒ _____ _____ : one to _____

1   What is the lecture mainly about?
    (A) How hormones send messages to cells
    (B) Hormones used for communication in the body
    (C) The function of the endocrine system
    (D) Relationships between the endocrine and nervous systems

2   How does the professor explain the way the endocrine system works?
    (A) By describing the messages it sends
    (B) By comparing it to a radio broadcast
    (C) By giving examples of hormones
    (D) By explaining the advantages of telephones

Listen and fill in the blanks.

Professor: The endocrine system is used by the body for communication. It's _____ _____ _____ _____ that produce hormones and use them to send messages. _____ _____ _____ the blood stream, these hormones can affect the activities of cells throughout the body. They help regulate _____ _____ _____ things, such as growth and eating... even the way you feel.

Student: But, um... isn't the nervous system _____ _____ communication in the body?

P: You're right. Both systems are used for communication, but they _____ _____ _____ _____. Think of the nervous system as a telephone network. Messages are sent from one cell to another, _____ _____ _____ _____. But _____ _____ _____ _____ _____ communicate with a large group of people all at once? Calling each of them one at a time would _____ _____ _____. But if you owned a radio station, you could _____ _____ _____ that everyone could hear _____ _____. This is sort of how the endocrine system works. It doesn't produce radio waves, of course, but it sends hormones _____ _____ _____ in much the same way.

LISTENING PRACTICE 02

ASTRONOMY

📋 **NOTE-TAKING**

Red dwarf stars

- _____ (100 times _____ than the _____)
- _____ life (burning fuel _____)
- Why _____ ?
  Because of _____ _____
  Like colors of a _____ (_____ > yellow > _____)

1   **What is the lecture mainly about?**

    (A) How red dwarf stars burn their fuel

    (B) Why red dwarf stars are not very hot

    (C) Different colors of stars in outer space

    (D) Characteristics of one group of stars

2   **Why does the professor mention colors of a fire?**

    (A) To introduce other stars that have different colors

    (B) To explain the relationship between colors and temperatures

    (C) To emphasize red dwarf stars can live a very long time

    (D) To give an example of an object that burns slowly

Listen and fill in the blanks.

Professor: Looking up into the night sky, all of the beautiful stars look _____ _____ _____ _____ to you and me. But the scientists who study these stars divide them into groups based on their _____ _____ _____. Red dwarf stars, for example, are _____ _____ _____ type of star. Compared to other stars, they're quite small... they _____ _____ _____ from about a hundred times smaller than the Sun to only a couple of times smaller. Red dwarfs _____ _____ _____ _____ _____, since they burn their fuel very slowly. And... well, does anyone know _____ _____ red dwarf stars red?

Student: Is it because they're so hot?

P: No... But that's a pretty good guess. The answer _____ _____ _____ temperature, but red dwarf stars are actually _____ _____ most other types of stars. Think about the colors of a fire. _____ _____ _____ of a fire, which is nearest to the source of fuel, glows blue. The middle part is yellow, and the coolest part of a fire, on the outer edge, _____ _____.

LISTENING PRACTICE 03

FILM STUDIES

📋 **NOTE-TAKING**

_____ _____ in films

; how much scene is shown

• _____ choose the right one for a _____ (like using _____ for _____)

① Close-up: shows _____ (_____)

② _____ shot: shows large area (_____)

③ _____ shot: shows _____ _____ (power & _____)

---

1   Why does the professor mention crayons?

    Ⓐ To give an example where a close-up shot is used

    Ⓑ To emphasize the importance of using the right shot size

    Ⓒ To show the difference between close-ups, long shots, and medium shots

    Ⓓ To explain how each shot produces a certain audience response

2   Indicate whether each of the following is related to close-ups, long shots, or medium shots.

Drag each phrase to the space where it belongs.

    Ⓐ Displays body language

    Ⓑ Creates a strong feeling

    Ⓒ Helps audience understand a scene

Close-up	Long shot	Medium shot

Listen and fill in the blanks.

Professor: Directors have many visual tricks they use _____ _____ _____ in their films. One of these is _____ _____ _____ their shots... that is to say, how much of the scene is shown _____ _____ _____. Shot size is an important tool for creating the proper mood, and directors must _____ _____ _____ _____ for each situation. You know... you might use a crayon to draw a picture, but you wouldn't use one to _____ _____ _____, would you?

Okay, a close-up, which shows _____ _____ an actor's face, can be used to create tension. A long shot, on the other hand, will show a large part of the area _____ _____ _____, perhaps a city street or forest. It doesn't create a strong mood like a close-up, but it can _____ _____ _____ _____ _____ a situation. Finally, a medium shot shows the actors from a comfortable distance that is similar to the way _____ _____ _____ _____. It's not great for _____ _____, but can easily show an actor's body language. Also, the position of the actors in a medium shot can also be used to _____ _____ _____ _____.

iBT PRACTICE

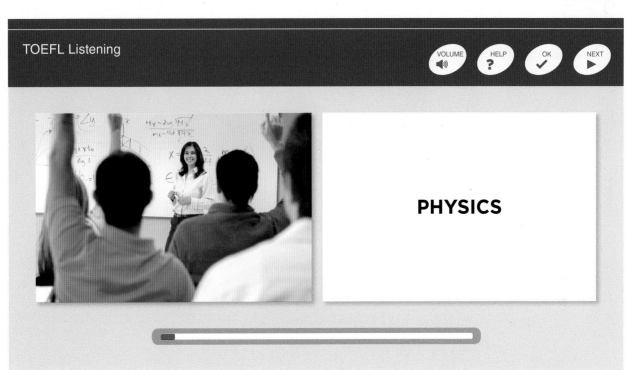

TOEFL Listening   VOLUME HELP OK NEXT

PHYSICS

📋 **NOTE-TAKING**

Q. Heat up a pan to _____℃ and add a drop of water?

• evaporate because it's the _____ _____

Q. Heat to _____℃?

• evaporate _____?

No. The drop would _____ ⇒ Leidenfrost effect

above _____℃(= Leidenfrost point) _____ of the drop becomes _____

∵ Steam prevents _____ _____

→ Water drop takes _____ to _____

1. What is the lecture mainly about?
   Ⓐ How heat is moved from one material to another
   Ⓑ What affects the boiling point of water
   Ⓒ The difference between the boiling and Leidenfrost points
   Ⓓ The Leidenfrost effect and its principles

2. How does the professor introduce the Leidenfrost effect?
   Ⓐ By correcting a common misunderstanding about the boiling point
   Ⓑ By mentioning her experience of cooking with a frying pan
   Ⓒ By letting the students predict what would happen in the given situation
   Ⓓ By explaining the proper frying temperature for cooking

3. Why doesn't water evaporate immediately at 200 degrees Celsius?
   Ⓐ Because steam prevents direct contact between the water and the pan
   Ⓑ Because the water moves so fast that it doesn't get enough heat
   Ⓒ Because heat disappears very quickly above 160 degrees Celsius
   Ⓓ Because the pan keeps the temperature below the boiling point

Listen again to part of the lecture. Then answer the question.

4. What does the professor mean when she says this: 🎧
   Ⓐ She believes the student doesn't understand her question.
   Ⓑ She is surprised at the student's answer.
   Ⓒ She thinks the student's answer is logical but wrong.
   Ⓓ She is not sure what the student is talking about.

Listen and fill in the blanks.

Professor: Okay, here's the situation: you're in the kitchen and you heat up a frying pan to 100 degrees Celsius. _____ _____ _____ _____ you placed a single drop of water onto the pan? Anyone?

Student: Um… it would bubble for a second, and then _____ _____ _____ _____. It would evaporate.

P: That's correct. It's because _____ _____ _____ of water is 100 degrees Celsius. So, what do you think would happen if we heated the pan _____ _____ 200 degrees and then placed the drop of water on it?

S: It would evaporate _____ _____ _____?

P: Well, you may think so, since it's _____ _____ _____ _____ the boiling point. But in reality, you would _____ _____ _____ _____. The drop _____ _____ _____ the surface of the pan for up to 20 seconds before it, um, evaporated. _____ _____ _____ _____ the Leidenfrost effect, named after the scientist who discovered it. Here's what happens… if the surface of the pan is hot enough, usually _____ _____ 160 degrees Celsius, we say that it has passed the Leidenfrost point. At this temperature, the bottom of the water drop will quickly turn into a gas, becoming steam. This steam will _____ _____ _____ _____ _____ from the pan to the upper part of the water drop. I mean… um, because of the steam, the process of heat transfer is _____ _____. As a result, the water drop _____ _____ to evaporate, even in temperatures higher than the boiling point. It _____ _____ _____, but it's true!

VOCABULARY REVIEW

A Choose the correct word for each definition.

mood	predict	glow	broadcast	polish

1. to make smooth and shiny: _____
2. an emotional state: _____
3. to make a guess about the future: _____
4. to shine or give off light: _____

B Choose the best word to explain the underlined word.

1. If something is <u>medium</u>, it is _____.
   - (A) physical
   - (B) logical
   - (C) average
   - (D) opposite

2. If something is <u>visual</u>, you can _____ it.
   - (A) see
   - (B) stick
   - (C) bounce
   - (D) use

3. If you give a <u>response</u> to something, you give your _____ to it.
   - (A) copy
   - (B) element
   - (C) tension
   - (D) reaction

C Choose the best word to complete each sentence. Change the form if necessary.

director	reflect	responsible	analogy	layer

1. As you grow older, you get more _____.
2. The _____ told the actors to show more emotion.
3. The cake had two _____ — one chocolate and one vanilla.
4. He drew a(n) _____ between orchestra and society.

D Choose the best phrase to complete each sentence.

1. Atmospheric pressure is _____ the liquid.
   - Ⓐ pressing down on
   - Ⓑ holding down
   - Ⓒ flattening out
   - Ⓓ smoothing out

2. He seems confident, but _____ he is very shy.
   - Ⓐ in question
   - Ⓑ in detail
   - Ⓒ in effect
   - Ⓓ in reality

3. To complete an experiment successfully, you should follow the process _____.
   - Ⓐ side by side
   - Ⓑ from time to time
   - Ⓒ step by step
   - Ⓓ all at once

E Choose the word or phrase that is closest in meaning to the underlined word.

1. I'm interested in learning about <u>ancient</u> cultures.
   - Ⓐ foreign
   - Ⓑ old
   - Ⓒ unknown
   - Ⓓ forgotten

2. The water will start to <u>bubble</u> when it gets really hot.
   - Ⓐ freeze
   - Ⓑ flow
   - Ⓒ boil
   - Ⓓ glow

3. The temperature in the building is <u>regulated</u> by the owners. We can't turn the heat up.
   - Ⓐ controlled
   - Ⓑ educated
   - Ⓒ evaporated
   - Ⓓ surrounded

4. The insects are usually a problem in summer, but they will <u>disappear</u> when it gets cold.
   - Ⓐ come along
   - Ⓑ gather around
   - Ⓒ go away
   - Ⓓ move in

F Choose the word that is the opposite of the underlined word.

1. There are important <u>similarities</u> between the two works.
   - Ⓐ discoveries
   - Ⓑ differences
   - Ⓒ relationships
   - Ⓓ distances

2. The <u>outer</u> layer of the banana is yellow.
   - Ⓐ top
   - Ⓑ inner
   - Ⓒ upper
   - Ⓓ bottom

Connecting Content

■ Connecting Content questions ask about the relationship between pieces of information from different parts of the conversation or lecture.

QUESTION TYPES

1. Question forms that require you to group or list

   · In the lecture, the professor describes X and Y. Put the following events in order. Drag each sentence to the space where it belongs.

   · Indicate whether each of the following is X or Y. Click in the correct box for each sentence.

2. Question forms that require you to synthesize information and draw a conclusion

   · What is the likely outcome of doing procedure X before procedure Y?

BASIC **DRILLS 01**

1-1 Indicate whether each of the following is related to the North Atlantic or the Pacific Ocean and Indian Ocean.
Click in the correct box for each phrase.

	The North Atlantic	The Pacific and Indian oceans
Ⓐ Cold deep currents flow.		
Ⓑ Warm surface currents flow.		
Ⓒ Water flows toward the poles.		
Ⓓ Dense water sinks.		

1-2 What does the professor mainly discuss?

Ⓐ How ocean currents circulate

Ⓑ How the ocean supports life

2-1 Put the following events in order.

Drag each sentence to the space where it belongs.

Ⓐ "V" was placed before "u" in the alphabet.

Ⓑ The letters "u" and "v" took on different sounds.

Ⓒ "U" started to come before "v" in the alphabet.

Ⓓ "V" was only used at the beginning of words.

1	
2	
3	
4	

2-2 How do you think the following words were spelled before the 18th century?

(1) us: _____

(2) evil: _____

Listen and fill in the blanks.

1.

Professor: The global conveyor belt is a system of ocean currents that _____ _____ _____ the world. While winds _____ _____ surface currents, deep currents _____ _____ _____ thermohaline circulation. At the poles, cold ocean water becomes _____ _____ _____ from ice formation. The dense water sinks, and then surface water moves in _____ _____ _____, thus creating a current. The conveyor belt begins in the North Atlantic. Cold water _____ _____ in the ocean to the south and resurfaces in the Pacific Ocean or Indian Ocean. As cold water _____ _____ _____, it brings carbon dioxide and nutrients to the surface. It supports the plankton and algae _____ _____ _____ _____ of the world's food chain. Now, the water travels in surface currents back to the North Atlantic. It takes 1,000 years to complete a circuit.

2.

Professor: The English language _____ _____ a lot of changes over time. For example, "u" and "v" were different forms of the same letter hundreds of years ago. _____ _____ _____ _____ a word, the "v" form was used, while the "u" form was _____ _____ _____. So, in those days, a word like "love" would have been spelled l-o-u-e, instead of l-o-v-e. There was, however, _____ _____ _____ _____ _____ the two letters made until the 18th century. At that time, the "v" form began to sound like [v] and the "u" form as [u]. When they were first separated, the letter "v" _____ _____ _____ "u" in the alphabet, although this order was _____ _____.

BASIC DRILLS 02

1-1 Indicate whether each of the following is related to the ozone layer or ground-level ozone.

Click in the correct box for each sentence.

	Ozone layer	Ground-level ozone
Ⓐ It is high up in the air.		
Ⓑ It damages life on the Earth.		
Ⓒ It blocks the Sun's harmful light.		
Ⓓ It is caused by pollution.		

1-2 Choose the sentence that is closest in meaning to what you hear. 🎧

Ⓐ The growth of trees and crops can be affected by ozone near the surface, and that ozone produces smog.

Ⓑ Smog causes ozone to form near the ground, which can affect the growth of trees and crops.

2-1 Indicate whether each of the following is related to the opera or the operetta.

Click in the correct box for each sentence.

	Opera	Operetta
Ⓐ It was sung in the local language.		
Ⓑ It was performed mainly by solo artists.		
Ⓒ It was popular among middle-class people.		
Ⓓ It was about serious and tragic stories.		

2-2 Choose the sentence that is closest in meaning to what you hear. 🎧

Ⓐ The audience didn't like them as much as operas because they were sung in a different language.

Ⓑ They were sung in the same language that the audience spoke, but operas weren't.

Listen and fill in the blanks.

1.

Professor: Whether ozone gas is "good" or "bad" depends on _____ _____ _____ in the air. _____ _____, in the upper atmosphere, is the same as the ozone layer. This ozone blocks dangerous UV rays and _____ _____ _____ _____ _____. Ozone becomes "bad" when it gets too close to the surface. Air pollution is the greatest cause of _____-_____ "bad" ozone. Bad ozone causes smog and can lead to _____ _____ _____, including lung disease. It can also cause less serious, but _____ _____, health problems like coughing and throat pain. The smog created by ground-level ozone can also _____ _____ _____ of trees and crops.

2.

Professor: In the 18th century, opera was very popular _____ _____ _____ _____. These operas usually had tragic stories and, importantly, they were only _____ _____ _____. Solo artists performed most of the songs, _____ _____ choruses or groups of singers. Among middle-class people, however, the operetta was _____ _____. Operettas weren't _____ _____ _____ operas... in fact, they were often quite funny. And, unlike operas, they were sung in the audience's native language.

Student: I guess that helped people _____ _____ _____ _____.

P: Of course. So, in an operetta, the characters could _____ _____ _____ the audience. Also, operettas often had choruses that would _____ _____ _____ the star performers.

LISTENING **PRACTICE 01**

LIBRARY

📋 **NOTE-TAKING**

Purpose: photocopy the book _____ _____

→ You have a _____ that hasn't been _____

I'll return it _____ & pay the _____

Photocopy?

→ _____ _____ the form

1   Why does the student go to the library?

Ⓐ To use a computer

Ⓑ To photocopy a book

Ⓒ To return a book

Ⓓ To meet his professor

2   Indicate whether each of the following is mentioned as something the student should do.

Click in the correct box for each phrase.

	Yes	No
Ⓐ Return a book		
Ⓑ Get a new ID card		
Ⓒ Pay a fine		
Ⓓ Fill out a form		
Ⓔ Call his professor		

Listen and fill in the blanks.

Student: Hi. I need to _____ _____ _____ from one of your books on reserve.

Librarian: All right. Can you _____ _____ _____ the name of your professor and the class that this is for?

S: Sure. It's for Professor Jacob's History of East Asia class.

L: Okay. And can I _____ _____ _____ _____, please?

S: Here you are.

L: Thank you. Hold on one moment, please. *[pause]* Hmm... I'm sorry, but you seem to have a book that hasn't been _____ _____. You already owe a $2 fine. If you don't return it this week, you'll have to pay _____ _____ _____.

S: Oh yeah! Sorry. I promise I'll return it tomorrow and _____ _____ _____. Um, does this mean I can't _____ _____ from the book on reserve today?

L: No, you still can. But you'll have to _____ _____ _____ _____ first.

S: Sure, no problem.

L: And, let's see... You said it was for Professor Jacob's class? The History of East Asia?

S: That's right.

L: Is this the book that _____ _____ _____?

S: That's it. Thanks so much for your help.

LISTENING PRACTICE 02

POLITICS

📋 NOTE-TAKING

U.S. governments

State governments (= _____ _____ governed themselves)

: weak → created _____ _____

⇨ Federal & state governments _____ _____

Federal: money system, _____ _____ , military

State: local business, _____, _____ _____ & safety

1   What does the professor mainly discuss?
   Ⓐ Reasons why governments should share their power
   Ⓑ Governments in the U.S. and their roles
   Ⓒ How to use national power in a country
   Ⓓ Federal governments and their importance

2   Indicate whether each of the following is related to federal government or state governments.
   Click in the correct box for each phrase.

	Federal government	State governments
Ⓐ Printing money		
Ⓑ Taking care of health issues		
Ⓒ Controling the army		
Ⓓ Running elections		

Listen and fill in the blanks.

Professor: America's _____ _____ _____ _____ was based on individual state governments. You know, America originally consisted of 13 colonies, and these colonies _____ _____. However, it was soon discovered that these state governments were _____ _____ _____ _____ _____. Instead, it was decided to create a federal government. The federal government controls _____ _____ _____. However, it shares _____ _____ _____ each of the state governments.

Let me give you some examples. It would be _____ _____ if each state had _____ _____ _____ of money, so the federal government controls a single form of money that is used by all the states. The federal government is also _____ _____ _____ things like international trade and the military. State governments, on the other hand, control local business, conduct elections, and are responsible for _____ _____ _____ _____.

So, as you can see, power in America _____ _____ _____ the federal and state governments.

LISTENING PRACTICE 03

GEOLOGY

📋 **NOTE-TAKING**

Weathering

: big rocks → _____ & _____

Causes of _____ weathering

① _____ : ice creates _____

② _____ : creates _____

③ _____ : rocks get _____ in heat

⇨ break apart

1   What is the lecture mainly about?
   Ⓐ Reasons why weather changes
   Ⓑ The meaning of physical and chemical weathering
   Ⓒ Effects of water on rock formations
   Ⓓ Different reasons for physical weathering

2   Indicate whether each of the following is related to physical weathering or not.
   Click in the correct box for each phrase.

	Yes	No
Ⓐ When water becomes ice inside of rocks		
Ⓑ When salt melts rocks		
Ⓒ When rocks become bigger or smaller due to temperature changes		
Ⓓ When rocks change into another type of rock		

Listen and fill in the blanks.

Professor: Who can tell me where _____ _____ _____ _____ _____? *[pause]* The answer is "weathering." Weathering turns big rocks into little rocks, and little rocks into sand and soil. You need to know that there are _____ _____ _____ _____, but we're only going to look at one today: physical weathering. Um, in this type of weathering, the rocks _____ _____ _____, only physically. That is, big rocks get smaller, and little rocks turn into even smaller rocks.

_____ _____ _____ _____ of physical weathering, but the most common is water. Water enters holes and _____ _____ _____. During very cold weather, the water turns into ice, which _____ _____ _____. Salt is another leading cause of physical weathering. Water often has some salt in it. _____ _____ _____ _____ _____, the salt remains. The salt creates pressure on the rocks. Changes _____ _____ also cause physical weathering. Rocks _____ _____ _____ in the sun and heat, then return to their normal size when it gets cooler. This damages rocks and will eventually cause them _____ _____ _____.

iBT PRACTICE

UNIT 06 CONNECTING CONTENT

TOEFL Listening

VOLUME · HELP · OK · NEXT

ARCHITECTURE

📋 **NOTE-TAKING**

Leaning Tower of Pisa

: Started to _____ when first 3 _____ were finished

→ Built next _____ floors parallel with the _____

→ Started to lean to the _____ / 2 more floors built

→ Holes made in _____ of tower and filled with _____

→ _____ earth to the south, then _____ earth from the north

121

1. What is the lecture mainly about?
   - (A) A new technique for building towers
   - (B) The reason why the Tower of Pisa leans
   - (C) The popularity of Italian architecture
   - (D) Attempts to correct the Tower of Pisa's lean

2. Put the following events in the order in which they occurred according to the lecture.
   Drag each sentence to the space where it belongs.
   - (A) Three floors were built at a different angle than the floors below them.
   - (B) A project to raise the tower's south side failed.
   - (C) The tower began to lean towards the north.
   - (D) Earth was removed from under the north side.
   - (E) Holes were made in the base of the tower.

1	
2	
3	
4	
5	

3. According to the professor, why did workers recently decide not to make the tower perfectly straight?
   - (A) They were not certain that it could be done safely.
   - (B) They did not want to damage Pisa's tourism industry.
   - (C) They could not add enough earth under the tower.
   - (D) They did not have enough money to finish the project.

Listen and fill in the blanks.

Professor: Many tourists visit Italy to see a tower that looks like it's falling over. Of course, I'm talking about the Leaning Tower of Pisa. Construction on the tower began in 1173.

Student 1: Um... when did it start to lean?

P: Good question. Finishing the first three floors _____ _____ _____. This is when the tower _____ _____. After that, work _____ _____ _____ _____. In 1275, a new team of builders took over. In order to fix the lean, they built the next three floors _____ _____ _____ _____ instead of with the other floors. But the tower started leaning _____ _____ _____, toward the south. Nevertheless, they finished the tower in 1350, and even then it was still leaning. It was left alone for a long time, but it was eventually _____ _____ _____ _____. So, in 1934, to strengthen the foundation, workers _____ _____ in the tower's base and filled them with cement. Unfortunately, this caused the tower to lean more. In 1995, workers started _____ _____ _____ the south side, to raise it. But they realized that this was making it lean more too, so they stopped. Finally, in 1999, they tried the opposite idea, and _____ _____ _____ the north side. This _____ _____ _____, and the tower was made 16 inches straighter.

Student 2: Professor... why didn't they just _____ _____ _____ _____?

P: Well, they could have. But then all those tourists who go to see the Leaning Tower of Pisa would have _____ _____ _____, right?

VOCABULARY REVIEW

A   **Choose the correct word for each definition.**

dense	pressure	reverse	govern	parallel

1. to officially control a country: _____
2. having parts that are close together: _____
3. running side by side and never crossing: _____
4. to turn in the opposite direction: _____

B   **Choose the best word to explain the underlined word.**

1. If something <u>melts</u>, it becomes a(n) _____.
   - (A) pressure
   - (B) air
   - (C) smog
   - (D) liquid

2. If something is <u>tragic</u>, it is _____.
   - (A) sad
   - (B) perfect
   - (C) responsible
   - (D) straight

3. If you <u>damage</u> something, you _____ it.
   - (A) examine
   - (B) spell
   - (C) harm
   - (D) limit

C   **Choose the best word to complete each sentence. Change the form if necessary.**

throat	leading	fine	upset	perform	undergo

1. The actors will _____ the show for the first time tonight.
2. If you are late returning your library book, you will have to pay a(n) _____.
3. I can't sing tonight. I have a pain in my _____.
4. He was _____ because he lost his job.
5. Smoking is the _____ cause of lung disease.

D Choose the best phrase to complete each sentence.

1. A healthy diet should _____ a variety of nutritious foods.
   Ⓐ get together   Ⓑ take away   Ⓒ consist of   Ⓓ break apart

2. I couldn't finish doing the dishes, so my brother _____.
   Ⓐ got back   Ⓑ took over   Ⓒ ran away   Ⓓ looked around

3. My sister is _____ a new company. She is the boss.
   Ⓐ in charge of   Ⓑ in the middle of
   Ⓒ on the other side of   Ⓓ by herself

E Choose the word or phrase that is closest in meaning to the underlined word.

1. There was a <u>crack</u> in the wall.
   Ⓐ break   Ⓑ stone   Ⓒ paint   Ⓓ color

2. Spanish is not my <u>native language</u>, but I speak it well.
   Ⓐ mother tongue   Ⓑ speech ability
   Ⓒ favorite subject   Ⓓ common saying

3. The kids were digging in the <u>earth</u> in the garden.
   Ⓐ planet   Ⓑ floor   Ⓒ soil   Ⓓ grass

4. They finally did it on their third <u>attempt</u>.
   Ⓐ day   Ⓑ aspect   Ⓒ try   Ⓓ class

F Choose the word that is the opposite of the underlined word.

1. I bought these tomatoes from a <u>local</u> farmer.
   Ⓐ individual   Ⓑ foreign   Ⓒ poor   Ⓓ diligent

2. He <u>blocked</u> the shot and his team won the game.
   Ⓐ scored   Ⓑ lost   Ⓒ missed   Ⓓ allowed

3. The teacher <u>separated</u> the two students because they were talking.
   Ⓐ rewarded   Ⓑ punished   Ⓒ praised   Ⓓ united

Inference

- Inference questions ask you about information that is suggested but not directly stated in the conversation or lecture.

- You will sometimes be asked to listen again to part of the conversation or lecture before answering the question.

QUESTION TYPES

· What will the student probably do next?

· What does the professor imply about X?

· What can be inferred about X?

· What does the professor imply when he/she says this: 🎧

BASIC DRILLS 01

Listen again to part of the lecture. Then answer the question.

1-1 What does the professor imply when she says this: 🎧
- Ⓐ Pollock is well known for a picture of the sky overhead.
- Ⓑ Pollock's paintings don't need to be laid down for exhibition.
- Ⓒ Pollock's works of art are more valuable than any other pictures.
- Ⓓ Pollock didn't want to exhibit his paintings in a gallery.

1-2 Why did some people want to lay Pollock's paintings on gallery floors?
- Ⓐ Because they thought the paintings were too big to hang on walls
- Ⓑ Because they wanted to appreciate the paintings the way they were created

2-1 What does the professor imply when he says this: 🎧
- Ⓐ It's not totally wrong to say that tulips come from the Netherlands.
- Ⓑ Many flowers other than tulips come from the Netherlands.
- Ⓒ No one knows why the Netherlands is famous for flowers.
- Ⓓ Many people wrongly think tulips are from the Netherlands.

2-2 Write T for True or F for False based on the lecture.
- (1) The Netherlands exports tulips to many countries. _____
- (2) "Tulip" means "flower" in Turkish. _____

127

Listen and fill in the blanks.

1.

Professor: The next painting is by Jackson Pollock. Pollock _____ _____ _____ called action painting. He'd take a large canvas, perhaps as big as _____ _____ _____, and lay it down on the floor. And then he... well, his method of painting _____ _____ _____ his entire body. He'd dip sticks into paint and use them to _____ _____ _____ onto his canvas as he walked around it. Some said his paintings _____ _____ _____ _____ in galleries because Pollock put them on the floor when he painted them. But think about it... after you take a picture of the sky overhead, you _____ _____ _____ on the ceiling to appreciate it.

2.

Professor: So, let's talk about tulips. I'm sure you're all _____ _____ tulips, right? But does anyone know _____ _____ _____ _____?

Student: They come from the Netherlands, don't they?

P: I knew you would say that. I'm sure many of you thought tulips _____ _____ _____ the Netherlands. But nothing _____ _____ _____ from the truth. Tulips actually _____ _____ Turkey. In fact, their name comes from the Turkish word for turban. They _____ _____ _____ the Netherlands in the 16th century, where they quickly _____ _____. These days, as I'm sure you know, the people of the Netherlands grow many tulips and export them to other countries _____ _____ _____ _____.

BASIC DRILLS 02

Listen again to part of the lecture. Then answer the question.

1-1 What does the professor imply when she says this: 🎧
- Ⓐ The surface of the Earth is too hard to dig.
- Ⓑ It is impossible to understand the Earth by digging.
- Ⓒ Digging is still the best way to study the Earth.
- Ⓓ Geologists have developed various methods of digging.

1-2 Choose the sentence that is closest in meaning to what you hear. 🎧
- Ⓐ When an earthquake occurs, seismic waves move through the ground.
- Ⓑ Earthquakes sometimes occur when seismic waves travel across the Earth.

2-1 What does the professor imply when he says this? 🎧
- Ⓐ The disease exchange affected Native Americans more than Europeans.
- Ⓑ The exchange happened before medicine was available in the New World.
- Ⓒ Native Americans should have been more prepared for European diseases.
- Ⓓ Europeans used the Native Americans' vulnerability to disease against them.

2-2 Choose the sentence that is closest in meaning to what you hear. 🎧
- Ⓐ The world economy improved because everyone wanted to buy items from overseas.
- Ⓑ Settlers in the New World boosted their economy by bringing Old World crops with them.

Listen and fill in the blanks.

1.

Professor: The Earth _____ _____ _____ : the crust, the mantle, the outer core, and the inner core. How do you think geologists have _____ _____ _____ ? Digging? Nice try, but the Earth is 4,000 miles _____ _____ _____ _____ . Anyone else? Okay… then I'll tell you. Geologists use seismic waves. This is not _____ _____ _____ , like digging, but it works better, and you don't sweat as much! Seismic waves _____ _____ _____ _____ during earthquakes. When they pass through different materials, their direction, motion, and speed _____ _____ _____ _____ . _____ _____ seismic waves, scientists have learned about the _____ _____ _____ that make up the Earth.

2.

Professor: Europeans arrived in the Americas in 1492. This started _____ _____ _____ of plants, animals, and diseases known as the "Columbian Exchange." New crops and animals _____ _____ , lifestyles, and the economy in the New World and the Old. Corn and potatoes became a major food in many countries and led to _____ _____ _____ in the Old World. To the New World, Europeans brought pigs, cows, chickens, and horses, as well as crops like sugar cane, wheat, bananas, and coffee. Massive _____ _____ _____ _____ worldwide, especially sugar, coffee, tobacco, and cotton, created new patterns of production and new global networks of trade.

The Columbian Exchange also _____ _____ _____ _____ results, such as the spread of disease. This tragic aspect was _____ - _____ , leading to the death of millions of Native Americans.

LISTENING PRACTICE 01

OFFICE HOURS

📋 **NOTE-TAKING**

Problem: Late for the _____!

→ You can't go inside

Want to meet _____ to _____ the exam

→ stop by at 12:30

    But you must get _____ from the _____ for _____

1   **What are the speakers mainly discussing?**

    Ⓐ Why the student is late for the exam

    Ⓑ Ways to change the school's policy

    Ⓒ Rescheduling the student's exam

    Ⓓ Changing to a different class

2   **What will the student probably do next?**

    Ⓐ Visit the dean and ask to take the exam later

    Ⓑ Study all night in order to pass the exam

    Ⓒ Drop the class and sign up for a new one

    Ⓓ Call his professor to schedule an appointment

Listen and fill in the blanks.

Student: *[out of breath]* Oh no! Please don't tell me the exam _____ _____

_____.

Teaching Assistant: I'm sorry, but it has. You're nearly 15 minutes late.

S: I know. My alarm _____ _____ _____ this morning. Can I go inside,

please?

A: I'm sorry, but you know the rules. Once the exam starts, _____ _____

_____ _____ _____ the classroom.

S: *[sadly]* Yes, I know. I guess I need _____ _____ _____ Professor

Griffin about this. When do you think I can meet with him?

A: _____ _____ _____ _____ around 12:30.

S: All right, I will. Do you think he'll _____ _____ _____ _____ my

exam?

A: Oh. I'm afraid that's not up to him. You'll have to _____ _____ _____

the dean of the department.

S: Really? Oh boy... Do you think the dean will _____ _____ _____ the

exam for later this week?

A: To be honest, the dean is quite strict _____ _____ _____ _____

school policy. You're going to have to work pretty hard to convince her.

S: Well, I guess I have to try. _____ _____ _____...

A: Good luck. I hope it all works out.

LISTENING PRACTICE 02

PSYCHOLOGY

📋 **NOTE-TAKING**

Contrast Effect

: evaluating the same thing _____ accd. to _____

e.g. ① hands in _____ & _____ water → _____ water

⇨ feel _____

② bad one next to good one ⇒ _____ one looks much better

③ $1,000 vs. $150 ⇒ $150 looks much _____

1 What is the lecture mainly about?

Ⓐ Reasons why we buy expensive products

Ⓑ A method of reasonable decision-making

Ⓒ How the contrast effect influences our judgment

Ⓓ Marketing tricks that make products look better

Listen again to part of the lecture. Then answer the question.

2 What does the professor imply when he says this: 🎧

Ⓐ Salespeople don't usually trick their customers.

Ⓑ Buying a $150 shirt is not a reasonable decision.

Ⓒ Expensive shirts shouldn't be washed in hot water.

Ⓓ Buying a $1,000 shirt is a better decision in this case.

Listen and fill in the blanks.

Professor: We'd like to believe we always _____ _____ _____. Unfortunately, it's not true. One of the reasons we can't _____ _____ is the contrast effect. We tend to evaluate the same thing differently _____ _____ _____ _____. For example... um, imagine you put your left hand in cold water and your right in hot water. And then you put both hands together into warm water. You know _____ _____ _____, right?

Student: My left hand will feel hot, but the right will feel cold.

P: Yes. _____ _____ _____ _____ even though they are in the same water. This kind of thing often happens. Let's see... _____ _____ _____ _____ how salespeople use the contrast effect? They put a poor quality product next to one that they want to sell in order to make the target product _____ _____ _____. Or they show you a $1,000 shirt first and then a $150 shirt. You are _____ _____ _____ the second one because it seems very cheap compared to the first one. But the truth is... the _____ _____ _____ _____ _____ again.

LISTENING **PRACTICE 03**

GEOLOGY

📋 **NOTE-TAKING**

Limestone cave formation

begins with _____ and _____ in the air → become _____

→ absorbed by soil (more CO_2 from _____ _____)

→ acidic water dissolves limestone (large _____ develops)

→ water _____ _____ rock & sand

→ _____ is formed

1   **What does the professor mainly discuss?**
   Ⓐ Chemical reactions in cave formation
   Ⓑ What makes limestone caves amazing
   Ⓒ Geological effects of acidic rainwater
   Ⓓ How limestone caves are created

2   **What can be inferred about limestone caves?**
   Ⓐ They are more commonly found where heavy rains fall.
   Ⓑ They are generally much larger than non-limestone caves.
   Ⓒ Not all of them are formed through chemical reactions.
   Ⓓ They are formed through both chemical and physical reactions.

Listen and fill in the blanks.

Professor: Take a look at this amazing photograph of a limestone cave. _____ _____ _____ _____ how this kind of cave forms?

Surprisingly, it begins in the air... specifically, it begins when two things _____ _____ _____ _____ _____ — rain and carbon dioxide. As rain falls from the sky, it absorbs carbon dioxide in the air, which causes it _____ _____ _____. When this rain reaches the earth, it _____ _____ _____ the soil, where it _____ _____ _____ carbon dioxide that has been produced by dead plants. If this water _____ _____ any limestone in the ground, it can form caves. _____ _____ _____ _____ the acidic water has a chemical reaction with the limestone. The water dissolves the limestone, causing _____ _____ _____ _____.

And that's not all water does. As the space in the limestone grows, underground water can _____ _____ these areas, washing away loose rock and sand. This causes the space to enlarge even further. _____ _____ _____ _____ over the course of hundreds of thousands — perhaps even millions — of years, and eventually _____ _____ _____ _____.

iBT PRACTICE

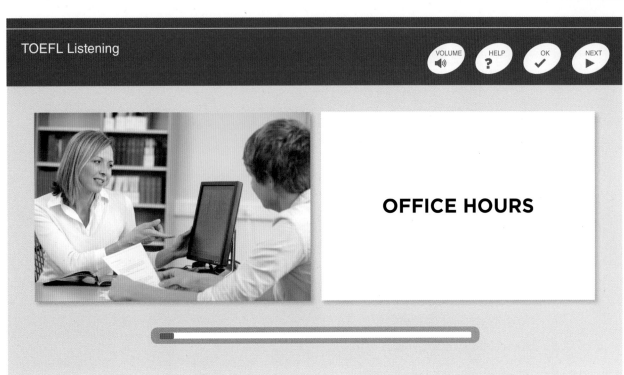

TOEFL Listening

VOLUME HELP OK NEXT

OFFICE HOURS

📋 **NOTE-TAKING**

Here for appointment to arrange _____ schedule

Performance: _____ GPA

Know about _____ program? – Have _____ about it

Rigorous, do not like to _____ students into it

But many benefits, especially for _____ _____

Main thing is the _____ :

– _____ pages

– Often meet with _____ advisor

– Senior year, present and _____ thesis

Students must join or not by the _____ of sophomore year

Take time to _____ about it, meet again later

137

1. What do the speakers mainly discuss?
   (A) Class schedules
   (B) Efficient methods of studying
   (C) Options for graduate school
   (D) Honors program requirements

2. What can be inferred about the student's academic performance?
   (A) He gets perfect grades.
   (B) He is steadily improving.
   (C) He does well in most classes.
   (D) He is the top student in his class.

3. According to the advisor, what is difficult about the thesis?
   (A) It takes a long time to complete.
   (B) It is long and must be defended.
   (C) It gets examined by other departments.
   (D) It involves giving several presentations.

4. What does the advisor imply when she says this: 🎧
   (A) The student can think about it until the next semester starts in fall.
   (B) The student needs to choose classes for the following year immediately.
   (C) The student must decide before registering for next year's classes.
   (D) The student is not eligible because he is already in his sophomore year.

Listen and fill in the blanks.

Student: Ms. Lewis? Hi, I'm here for my appointment.

Advisor: Oh, hi, Peter. We need to _____ _____ _____ _____ for the fall, right?

S: That's right.

A: Good. And I see you have a 4.0 GPA. Very nice!

S: Yeah. I'm pretty happy about it.

A: You should be. I want to ask you something. Do you know about the honors program here?

S: Um… I've heard about it. Do you think _____ _____ _____?

A: Hmm… Well, it is rigorous. As an advisor, I don't like to push students into it. But it has _____ _____ _____ _____. It's especially good if you want to go to _____ _____.

S: Oh, I didn't know that. But it's more difficult?

A: It's quite a bit more work. The main thing is your thesis. It needs to be 30 pages. And, well, _____ _____ _____ _____. You'll have to have frequent meetings with an honors advisor. There is one for every major. In your senior year, you'll need to _____ _____ _____ your thesis. Now, even normal classes are demanding. And this is a step up.

S: I see.

A: It's _____ _____, but here's the thing. Students have to apply by the beginning of their sophomore year. And, um, and it would _____ _____ _____ you could take.

S: Ah, okay. Can I _____ _____ _____ to think about it?

A: Yes, that's what I was going to suggest. Think it over for a day or so. Then we can meet again and talk about class registration.

S: Okay, that sounds good.

VOCABULARY REVIEW

A **Choose the correct word for each definition.**

geologist	reschedule	hunter	alter	arrange

1. to change the time of a planned event or appointment: _____
2. to cause the characteristics of something to change: _____
3. one who tracks and kills animals: _____
4. to organize or make plans for a future event: _____

B **Choose the best word to explain the underlined word.**

1. If you give someone underlined permission to do something, you _____ it.
   (A) drop (B) allow (C) nsure (D) dip

2. If a graduate program is rigorous, it is _____.
   (A) demanding (B) strict (C) harsh (D) thorough

3. If your art is in an exhibition, it is on _____.
   (A) profit (B) ceiling (C) canvas (D) display

C **Choose the best word to complete each sentence. Change the form if necessary.**

earthquake	defend	target	sweat	blanket

1. I _____ so much on hot summer days.
2. The advertisement was designed to appeal to the _____ market.
3. Their home was destroyed in a(n) _____.
4. I will _____ my mayster's thesis in computer science.

D **Choose the best phrase to complete each sentence.**

1. You're welcome to _____ our cabin while we're away.
   - (A) make use of
   - (B) sign up for
   - (C) run for
   - (D) leave out

2. Feel free to _____ my office anytime.
   - (A) stop by
   - (B) go off
   - (C) figure out
   - (D) make up

3. _____ math, she is a genius.
   - (A) At the top of
   - (B) Next to
   - (C) In favor of
   - (D) When it comes to

E **Choose the word or phrase that is closest in meaning to the underlined word.**

1. We have to write an essay on the significance of the Korean War.
   - (A) disadvantage
   - (B) determination
   - (C) importance
   - (D) component

2. The only reasonable thing to do is call the police.
   - (A) strict
   - (B) sensible
   - (C) amazing
   - (D) foolish

3. Tea originated in China.
   - (A) started
   - (B) grew
   - (C) was banned
   - (D) was loved

4. He has some valuable stamps in his collection.
   - (A) foreign
   - (B) rare
   - (C) precious
   - (D) surprising

F **Choose the word that is the opposite of the underlined word.**

1. We export goods to several countries around the world.
   - (A) import
   - (B) sell
   - (C) trade
   - (D) donate

2. The movie has moments of unintentional comedy.
   - (A) incidental
   - (B) authorized
   - (C) designed
   - (D) anticipated

Actual
Practice
Test

ACTUAL
PRACTICE
TEST **01**

ACTUAL
PRACTICE
TEST **02**

ACTUAL PRACTICE TEST 01

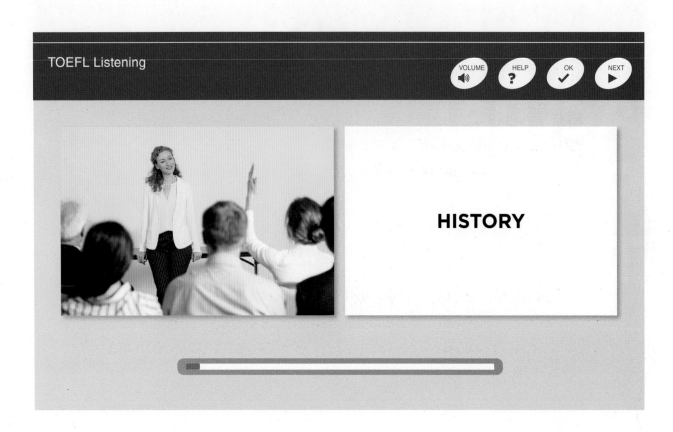

📋 NOTE-TAKING

The Industrial Revolution

• Why it started in _____ _____

① Geography: _____ _____

            _____ & waterways

② Social situation: labor forces in cities ↑

          ∵ new farming _____

        → _____ lost jobs and went to cities

③ Political & economic conditions:

• No _____ in GB

• Protecting _____ _____ & good _____ _____

TOEFL Listening

VOLUME   HELP   OK   NEXT

1. What is the lecture mainly about?

    Ⓐ The social impact of the Industrial Revolution

    Ⓑ The reasons the Industrial Revolution began in Great Britain

    Ⓒ The role Great Britain played in the world during the 18th century

    Ⓓ The changes the Industrial Revolution brought to Europe

2. What does the professor say about the key features of Great Britain's geography?
Click on 2 answers.

    Ⓐ It is located close to other countries.

    Ⓑ It is suitable for water travel.

    Ⓒ It has important natural resources.

    Ⓓ It has few hills or mountains.

3. According to the professor, why did country people participate in the Industrial Revolution?

    Ⓐ They could no longer make a living as farmers.

    Ⓑ They could not afford to buy new farming technologies.

    Ⓒ The demand for farm products fell.

    Ⓓ The government ordered them to move to cities.

4. Indicate whether each of the following is mentioned as political and economic conditions in Great Britain.
Click in the correct box for each sentence.

	Yes	No
Ⓐ They became stable after a few wars.		
Ⓑ Economic activities were well supported by the government.		
Ⓒ Great Britain regulated the economy with a banking system.		
Ⓓ The government tried to protect the rights of inventors.		

ACTUAL PRACTICE TEST 02

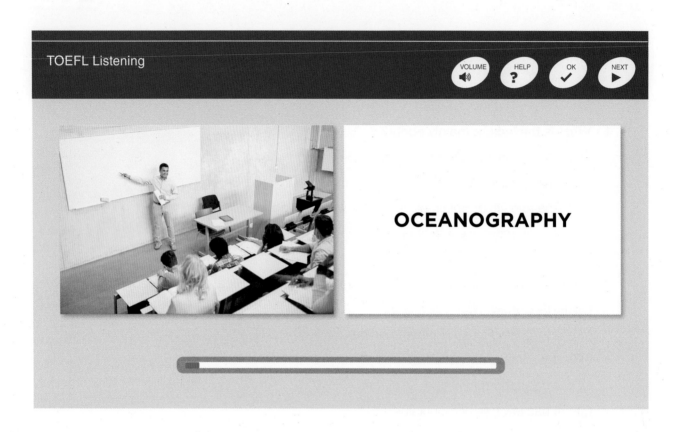

OCEANOGRAPHY

📋 NOTE-TAKING

Some parts of the ocean are _____ than others

(average salinity = _____ ppm = _____% salt)

Why?

① _____ → salinity ↑ (e.g. _____ oceans)

② _____ → salinity ↓

③ Addition of _____ _____ → salinity ↓

④ _____ _____ → salinity ↓ (e.g. _____ oceans)

5. What is the lecture mainly about?

(A) Ways to measure the salinity of seawater

(B) The effect of evaporation on seawater salinity

(C) Changes in the salinity of seawater

(D) Places where the salinity of seawater is changing

6. Indicate whether each of the following is related to high salinity or low salinity.
Click in the correct box for each phrase.

	High salinity	Low salinity
(A) Evaporation		
(B) Precipitation		
(C) Ice melting		
(D) Inflow of fresh water		

7. What can be inferred about the salinity of seawater?

(A) It is determined by changes in water quantity.

(B) It affects the climate of coastal regions.

(C) It varies because the amount of salt doesn't stay the same.

(D) The average salinity has been increased by global warming.

8. Why does the professor say this: 🎧

(A) To further clarify a point

(B) To get back to the topic of the lecture

(C) To review the previous lecture

(D) To emphasize an important point

Answer Keys
& Audio Scripts

UNIT 01 Main Idea

NOTE

⌐ *Highlighting and bold types respectively indicate the first and second repeated part in Replay Questions.*

⌐ *Underlined phrases show the answers of Dictation in Listening Practice.*

BASIC DRILLS 01

p. 15

1-1. Ⓐ 1-2. Ⓑ 2-1. Ⓒ 2-2. (1) eternity
(2) humans (3) God

1.

Listen to part of a lecture in a biology class.

Professor: Most people think that animals hibernate to stay warm and sleep through the winter. In fact, hibernation is a state where body functions are extremely slowed down. To slow their metabolisms, hibernating animals cool their bodies by 5 to 10 °C on average.

Animals hibernate for a few different reasons. First, hibernation is typically linked to seasonal changes that limit food supplies. Put simply, hibernation is a means of energy conservation. Of course, some animals hibernate in winter. But some animals have to save energy in the summer. Recent studies have even suggested another reason: protection. When hibernating, animals do not move, make sounds, or produce smells. Therefore, they are hard for predators to find. So, as you can see, hibernation is not simply sleep.

2.

Listen to part of a lecture in an art class.

Professor: Let's move on to the next painting. *The Starry Night* is Van Gogh's most famous painting, and perhaps his greatest. It shows a night sky with stars and a quiet town with a church. Also, there are, umm... cypress trees overlooking the town, which are quite impressive.

Student: Do the cypress trees have any special meaning?

P: Oh, yes. Some say that the cypress is a symbol of eternity. In this painting, they are connecting earth and sky, which are symbols of humans and God. From this point of view, the whole picture could have a religious meaning such as... um, perhaps our desire to reach God.

BASIC DRILLS 02

p. 17

1-1. Ⓐ 1-2. Ⓑ 2-1. Ⓓ 2-2. Ⓐ

1.

Listen to part of a lecture in an astronomy class.

Professor: Have you heard about the Hubble Space Telescope? It's a very special telescope which is in orbit around the Earth. Many scientists think the Hubble is one of the most effective telescopes. What I mean here by effective is... the Hubble helps us to see space objects more clearly.

Student: Why is that? Does it have better lenses or something?

P: Maybe. But think about where it is. It is outside the atmosphere, while other telescopes are on the ground. The atmosphere blurs the view from the ground, so scientists can't see objects clearly with other telescopes. However, with the Hubble, scientists can get a clear view of space objects.

2.

Listen to part of a lecture in an economics class.

Professor: Disposable income is a standard term in economics. It sounds complicated, but its meaning is really quite simple. Money earned minus taxes equals disposable income. This is easy to explain. Let's say that you earn $100 per week, and you pay 20% in taxes — 20% of $100 is $20. This is what you will have to pay in taxes to the government. Take your $100 weekly salary and lower it by $20. The result is $80. Thus, $80 is what you have left from your weekly salary, after paying taxes. This is your disposable income.

LISTENING PRACTICE 01

p. 19

1. Ⓒ 2. Ⓓ

📋 NOTE-TAKING

Purpose: Look for part-time jobs
– took a job in library, but it doesn't pay well
– need another job that offers more money
  (even off-campus)
⇒ Let you know by tomorrow afternoon

Listen to a conversation between a student and an adviser in a Career Service Center.

Adviser: Hi. Welcome to the Career Center. Are you Stephanie?

Student: That's right. I have an appointment for 11 o'clock.

A: Of course. Have a seat. *[pause]* So what did you want to discuss today?

S: Well, I was interested in finding out about available part-time jobs.

A: *[surprised]* Oh. Really?

S: Yes. Is there something wrong?

A: No... It's just that it's a little late in the semester to be looking for a job. Most of the open positions were filled weeks ago.

S: Yes, I realize that. I actually took a job with the school library a couple of weeks ago. Unfortunately, it doesn't pay very well. I really need to earn more money.

A: I see. So you're planning to quit your present job?

S: Yes. I'd prefer to leave this job and find another that can offer me more money. I'd be willing to do anything. I'd even work off-campus, if necessary.

A: All right, Stephanie. I'll look into what jobs are still available and let you know by tomorrow afternoon.

S: Thanks a lot.

LISTENING PRACTICE 02   p. 21

1. Ⓑ   2. Ⓓ

📋 **NOTE-TAKING**

Products for small, focused groups
→ niche market
e.g. scissors for the left-handed

For success: meet the needs
e.g. computers for students vs. office workers
(game, podcasting vs. office software)

Listen to part of a lecture in a marketing class.

Professor: Most products and services are designed for large groups of people. But sometimes companies try to sell their products only to a small, focused group. This special market is called a niche market. Let's see... how many of you are left-handed? *[pause]* When you use normal scissors, how does it feel?

Student: Not very good. I have to hold them in a strange way. It's uncomfortable to use my left hand.

P: That's right. Normal scissors are for right-handed people. However, there's a niche market — in this case, a market of left-handed people. If a company sells special scissors for these people, this is niche marketing. Niche products don't appeal to the majority of people, but they still have their own market, so they can earn money.

However, not every niche product earns money. For successful niche marketing, there's an important rule to keep in mind: meet the needs of the market. If a company wants to produce a computer for young college students, their computers must be different from computers for office workers. They might have... um, maybe special software for online games and podcasting rather than traditional office software.

LISTENING PRACTICE 03   p. 23

1. Ⓑ   2. Ⓐ, Ⓓ

📋 **NOTE-TAKING**

How can icebergs float on water?
iceberg = ice cube
① Density: water > ice
        1kg/L   0.99kg/L
② Salinity of seawater: salty → high density

Listen to part of a lecture in a physics class.

Professor: Have you ever wondered how it is possible for something as big as an iceberg to float on water? The answer is simple, in fact, if you think of an iceberg as nothing more than a really big ice cube. Ice cubes, of course, float on water. This is because ice has a different density from water. So what does that mean? Let me put it this way — a liter of water weighs one kilogram, which means the density of water is one kilogram per liter. But when you weigh a liter of ice cubes, you'll find that they weigh 0.99 kilograms, making the density of ice cubes 0.99 kilograms per liter. So icebergs, which are less dense than water, can float on water.

The salinity of seawater also helps icebergs float. Salinity is a measure of how salty water is, and it affects water density. As you know, seawater is quite salty, and it has a high density, about, umm... 1.02 kilograms per liter. As a result, it is even easier for an iceberg to float on seawater.

1. (A)   2. (C)   3. (B)   4. (D)

📋 NOTE-TAKING

Otters

River otters	Sea otters
Live in many places	Live in the ocean
Narrow face, webbed toes, longer tails	Paws – paddle shape
Come onto land	Spend most time in water
Small family 3~4 pups	Large group 1 pup

Listen to part of a lecture in a zoology class.

Professor: Today we'll be talking about otters, class. And in North America, there are two types — river otters and sea otters. As you've probably already guessed, sea otters live in the ocean. Okay... well, it's not so easy with river otters... they don't just live in rivers. Uh... they're found near many bodies of fresh water... rivers, streams, lakes... but they also live in the sea near the coast. So river otters and sea otters can actually share a habitat. And, well... this can make it hard to tell them apart.

Luckily, though, there are some big differences between the two. First of all... their bodies. **Q4** 🎧 River otters have narrower faces than sea otters. Also, a sea otter's rear paws are shaped like a paddle, but a river otter's have webbed toes. Oh... and one more — river otters have longer tails.

But what if you can't see their faces, paws, or... tails? You might still be able to, um, identify an otter... by its behavior. You see, sea otters spend almost all their time in the water, and they like to float around on their backs. River otters, though, come onto land all the time... especially to eat. And when they swim, they like to move around a lot. And lastly... there's group size. Sea otters like to stay in large groups, while, uh, river otters live in small family units. On the other hand, female river otters give birth to three or four pups at once, but female sea otters... they have only one at a time.

A 1. habitat   2. eternity   3. review   4. narrow
      5. salinity
B 1. (B)   2. (D)   3. (B)
C 1. left-handed   2. discovery   3. cube
      4. offered
D 1. (C)   2. (D)   3. (C)
E 1. (D)   2. (D)   3. (B)   4. (A)
F 1. (B)   2. (B)

p. 31

BASIC DRILLS 01

1-1. C   1-2. (1) T (2) F   2-1. D   2-2. B

1.

Listen to part of a lecture in a biology class.

Professor: There are, um, three types of blood cells: red blood cells, white blood cells, and platelets. Today we're, ahem, going to study red blood cells. First, their shape… uh, they are shaped like flattened disks. And their main job is to deliver oxygen to our bodies. How? Red blood cells pick up oxygen in the lungs and distribute it to the tissues as the blood travels through the body. Another thing we need to know is their life span. Each red blood cell lives for about four months. So, um, every day the body produces new cells to replace the ones that die.

2.

Listen to part of a lecture in a psychology class.

Professor: You probably know that first impressions are very important. It's true not only when you meet a person but also when you hear about a person. In an experiment, a group of people heard a series of words that described a person. Then they were supposed to decide whether that person was good or bad. First, they were told that Person A is smart, diligent, and stubborn. After that, they heard that Person B is stubborn, diligent, and smart. In fact, the words used to describe Person A and Person B were the same except for the order in which they were given. But the result was surprising. Most people had a better impression of Person A than Person B.

BASIC DRILLS 02

p. 33

1-1. B   1-2. B   2-1. B, D   2-2. B

1.

Listen to part of a lecture in an astronomy class.

Professor: Mars resembles Earth more than it resembles any other planet. Like Earth, Mars has four seasons: spring, summer, fall, and winter. But, um, the seasons on Mars are longer. Another thing: Each day is 24 hours and 39 minutes on Mars, which is — ahem — very close to Earth's 24-hour days. What was the other thing I wanted to mention? Oh yes, its temperature. Mars' temperature is similar to Earth's. Although Mars is much colder, with a range from about −113 °C to 20 °C, its temperature is still more like Earth's than any of the other planets.

2.

Listen to part of a lecture in a music class.

Professor: Flamenco is a passionate, deeply emotional art form that combines singing, guitar playing, and dancing. The essence of flamenco is the song. Flamenco songs fall into three categories: profound songs, intermediate songs, light songs. Each has its own characteristic rhythm and lyrics. The profound song, or deep song, based on a complex 12-beat rhythm, is the oldest form. It deals with profound emotions. Common themes include death, sorrow, despair, and anger. The intermediate song is less complex and incorporates other Spanish music styles. It is more lively and is often accompanied by guitars, castanets, and hand clapping. The light song is the simplest of the three styles. It has a quick, light rhythm and deals with lighter themes, such as love and humor.

LISTENING PRACTICE 01

p. 35

1. C   2. D

📋 NOTE-TAKING

Overdue fine
- Two weeks late
- Late fee: 25 cents a day per item / in total $21
Reservation
- All the copies checked out
- The earliest copy due back in three weeks
Interlibrary Services
- Receive an email when the book is available for pickup
- Register for an appointment to pick it up

Listen to a conversation between a student and a librarian.

Student: Hi. I have some books to return. Unfortunately, they're late.

Librarian: Okay. Let me take a look at them.

S: Here you go.

L: These are all two weeks late. The fee is 25 cents per day. And that's for each late book. So your late fees come to $21.

S: All right. *[Pause]* Could you also help me with something else? I was looking for a book, but I couldn't find it. Could you check if you have it? Here's the title and author.

L: Let's see. *[Pause]* Sorry. All our copies have been checked out.

S: That's too bad. Is it possible to reserve a copy?

L: Sure. Just give me your name and email address. We'll notify you when a copy is returned.

S: Thanks, I appreciate it. When do you think that will be?

L: Let's have a look... The earliest copy is due back in three weeks.

S: Three weeks? That's too long! I need it for a report.

L: Well, you can try Interlibrary Services on our website. You should be able to get it from another library sooner.

S: That's great. I haven't used that service before. I need to request that book right away.

L: If you do, you'll receive a notice by email when the book is available for pickup. There will also be a link to a page where you can make an appointment to pick it up.

S: Thank you so much.

LISTENING PRACTICE 02

p. 37

1. Ⓒ 2. Ⓑ, Ⓓ

NOTE-TAKING

Thermometer
; thermo → heat, meter → measure
Liquids change volume (cold → ↓, warm → ↑)
Q. liquid = water?
A. No, freezes below zero
→ Mercury: not freezing, sensitive to temperature changes

Listen to part of a lecture in a physics class.

Professor: A thermometer is a tool that measures the temperature of things. Its name is made up of two smaller words: "thermo," meaning heat, and "meter," meaning to measure.

The basic principle behind thermometers is that liquids will change their volume with changes in their temperature. At cold temperatures, their volume will decrease. As they get warmer, their volume will increase. These changes are small, so you wouldn't see them in something such as... say a glass of milk. But the liquid in thermometers is kept in a very thin tube, which makes these changes much easier to see.

Student: So, what kind of liquid is used in thermometers? Is it water?

P: Early thermometers used water. But water freezes below zero and that's a big problem, isn't it? Instead, mercury is generally used, which, um, solves the freezing problem. In addition, it is sensitive to changes in temperature, and increases or decreases with these changes. Therefore, the slightest change in temperature is easily measured with a thermometer.

LISTENING PRACTICE 03

p. 39

1. Ⓓ 2. Ⓑ, Ⓓ

NOTE-TAKING

Prisoner's Dilemma
Situation: criminal A, B
① If A & B don't confess → 1-year sentences
② If A & B confess → 5-year sentences
③ If A confesses & B doesn't
→ A: free, B: 10-year sentences
⇒ A & B don't trust each other
& concerned with own interests
∴ Both confess & get 5-year sentences

Listen to part of a lecture in a philosophy class.

Professor: The prisoner's dilemma is a classic example of game theory, which explains decision-making behavior. In the prisoner's dilemma, two criminals, A and B, are put into two cells after they commit a crime together. The police know they committed the crime but still need more evidence. So they tell criminal A this — if both A and B don't confess their crime, they'll get 1-year sentences. If neither A nor B confesses to the crime, they'll both get 1-year sentences. However, if A confesses while B doesn't confess, A will be set free and B will get a 10-year sentence. The police tell criminal B the same thing.

Student: So, the best case scenario is that... um, neither of them confesses and both get 1-year sentences.

P: Yes. If A and B trust each other, they can get minimum sentences. But neither is sure whether the other will confess or not. Besides, each wants to walk free and is only concerned with his own interest. As a result, they both confess and get 5-year sentences! That's the prisoner's dilemma. It shows that... without trust, well, each person will think only of themselves, which can lead to the worst outcome of all.

iBT PRACTICE

1. Ⓒ   2. Ⓑ   3. Ⓒ, Ⓓ   4. Ⓓ

📋 NOTE-TAKING

Go to graduate school or find a job?
– Go to graduate school
– Not sure about which programs
Pros and cons of dual degree programs
– Ask herself whether or not to pursue a dual degree
Set up a time to discuss MBA programs

Listen to a conversation between a student and a professor.

Student: Hi, Dr. Connelly. Do you have a minute?

Professor: Certainly, Anna. Why don't you sit down?

S: Well, I need your advice. You know that next semester is my last one. Then I'll graduate, and I'm not sure what to do.

P: Ah, yes. Well, that is a big step, and there are a lot of options to consider. I suppose you're already committed to business as your field.

S: Yes, I love this field.

P: Then, mainly, you have to decide if you're going to look for a job or go to graduate school. Have you thought about that?

S: I have, and I think I want to go to graduate school. But I am also interested in communication programs. I believe strategic communication skills are more important than ever in business.

P: I couldn't agree with you more. Um ... Some schools offer dual degree programs. You might find one that offers both MBA and communication degrees.

S: That sounds great.

P: Hmm ... with a dual degree, you'll broaden your knowledge and have more chances in your career path. Q4 🎧 However, you will need to stay longer in school. It will also require a lot of money. Above all, are you equally passionate about both fields?

S: Um ... I think I need to ask myself if a dual degree is right for me.

P: Well, why don't we set up a time to talk more? You could consider if you'll pursue a dual degree or not, and I'll suggest a few MBA programs.

S: That would be so helpful!

VOCABULARY REVIEW

A 1. pursue   2. thermometer   3. require
4. notify   5. sentence

B 1. Ⓐ   2. Ⓓ   3. Ⓑ   4. Ⓒ

C 1. passionate   2. graduated   3. life span
4. resembles

D 1. Ⓒ   2. Ⓒ   3. Ⓐ

E 1. Ⓒ   2. Ⓓ   3. Ⓒ   4. Ⓑ

F 1. Ⓑ   2. Ⓒ   3. Ⓓ

Actual Practice Test 1

01

pp. 48~49

1. Ⓒ   2. Ⓑ   3. Ⓐ   4. Ⓑ   5. Ⓒ

📋 NOTE-TAKING

Problem: Can't get the window to shut
– Why did you open it?
Was hot because of heating system
Bigger problem: Radiator blew up! → steam & rusty water
How long will it take to fix?
→ take a while
I will stay with uncle tonight
→ Okay, I'll fix it ASAP

Listen to a conversation between a student and a janitor.

Student: Excuse me, Mr. Edwards. Remember me? Amy from room 204?

Janitor: Ah, yes. I fixed your window last week. Don't tell me it's stuck again!

S: Well, actually, it is. I opened it last night, but then I couldn't get it to shut.

J: Why did you open that window in the first place? It's the middle of January.

S: You know how the heating system is in this dormitory. Sometimes my room gets really hot in the middle of the night. Anyway, the window isn't the reason I came here. I've got a bigger problem.

J: A bigger problem? Uh-oh. What happened?

S: Q4 🎧 Um, I think my radiator blew up last night.

J: Blew up? What exactly do you mean?

S: Well, it made this loud noise and a lot of steam came shooting out of it. And now there's rusty water on the floor.

J: **Oh, boy. Rusty isn't good.** [pause] All right, give me a few minutes to gather my tools, and then I'll head up to your room.

S: Okay. Q5 🎧 Um, do you have any idea how long it might take to fix everything?

J: Well, the window isn't a problem. I can fix that right away. But I'm not so sure about the radiator. I'll have to take a look at it first, but I'm pretty sure it's going to take a while. Why don't you come see me in a couple of hours? I should know for sure by then.

S: Well, I was just about to call my aunt and uncle who live nearby. Maybe I should tell them I need to stay there

tonight. **But I need to ask them now, so my uncle can pick me up on his way home from work.**

J: All right, all right. I think it's safe to say that your radiator won't be fixed until tomorrow morning at the earliest.

S: Okay. So I guess I'll ask to stay with them tonight.

J: That would be best. I'll try to get your room fixed up as soon as possible.

S: Thank you. I'll come by tomorrow and see how it's going.

02

pp. 50~51

6. Ⓑ   7. Ⓓ   8. Ⓓ   9. Ⓐ

📋 NOTE-TAKING

Muybridge: father of the motion picture
Discussion: Does a horse lift all its legs off the ground
　　　　　　 when it runs?
→ photographed a running horse with 24 cameras
Later, worked on other projects
→ helped Edison invent motion picture camera

Listen to part of a lecture in an art history class.

Professor: Class, can you tell me who invented the motion picture... uh, the movie?

Student 1: It was Thomas Edison, wasn't it?

P: I thought you might say that. It's a good guess, but it's not quite right. It's true that Edison invented the first, um, motion picture camera. And also the first machine that played motion pictures. But art historians say a photographer named Eadweard Muybridge is really "the father of the motion picture."

　Let me tell you why. It was 1872, and there was a big discussion going on. People wanted to know whether, um, whether a horse ever lifts all of its legs off the ground at once when it runs. And... well, as you know, horses are very fast. So it was impossible to figure this out just by watching a horse. Anyway, Muybridge was a photographer working in California at the time. Leland Stanford, who was the, the governor of California... he hired Muybridge to answer this question. And how do you think he did it?

Student 2: Q9 🎧 Um... it seems like the easiest way would be to film a running horse with a motion picture camera. But you already said, uh, Thomas Edison invented that. So Muybridge obviously didn't have one.

P: You're right. He didn't have a motion picture camera. But he didn't need one. Instead, to photograph the horse in motion, he set up a row of 24 still cameras. This row was, um, next to where the horse was running. Muybridge also... he developed a system to make each camera go off exactly as the horse passed it. So, at the end, he had a series of 24 pictures showing different stages of the horse's running motion. And in some of the pictures, you could clearly see the horse with all four legs off the ground.

Okay, now, this wasn't exactly a motion picture like we have today. It was just a short series of still photographs. But Muybridge's work on this... and other projects too, um, his work really helped Thomas Edison invent the motion picture camera. That's why historians call Eadweard Muybridge "the father of the motion picture."

UNIT 03 Function

BASIC DRILLS 01   p. 55

1-1. C   1-2. (1) T (2) F   2-1. D   2-2. A

1.

Listen to part of a lecture in a physics class.

Professor: Generally, we do not clearly distinguish mass from weight. However, they are totally different. Mass is how much matter an object contains. It is the same wherever you are. On the other hand, weight is a measurement of how hard gravity is pulling at the mass. So, your weight depends on how much gravity is acting on you at the moment. Here's a question. What would your weight be on the Moon? **Remember that the gravity of the Moon is one sixth of that of Earth.**

Student: I would weigh six times less than on Earth, right?

P: Right. But remember that mass is always the same whether you're on Earth or on the Moon.

2.

Listen to part of a lecture in an art history class.

Professor: The Federal Art Project, known as the FAP, was created during the New Deal to provide artists with jobs during the Depression. Participating artists were paid $23.50 a week, as long as they created one major work of art or spent enough time working on a project.

Student: Did it work?

P: Well... by 1936, more than 5,000 artists had joined, and that number probably doubled over the eight years of the project. It produced a total of more than 100,000 easel paintings, 17,000 sculptures, as well as nearly 300,000 fine prints. The final cost was more than $35,000,000. **Do I need to explain more?**

BASIC DRILLS 02

p. 57

1-1. Ⓑ   1-2. Ⓑ   2-1. Ⓑ   2-2. Ⓑ

1.

Listen to part of a lecture in a biology class.

Professor: Spiders have poor vision, unable to see more than darkness, light, and basic shapes, but they do have a very good sense of touch. By sensing vibrations, they are able to understand what is happening around them. 🎧 When their web shakes, for example, they can tell if it was caused by the wind or by an insect they can eat. This is because insects cause rough vibrations, while the wind causes smooth vibrations. **And** that's not all. When a male spider visits the web of a female spider to mate, he sends her special vibrations so she knows who he is and why he's there.

2.

Listen to part of a lecture in a literature class.

Professor: We've been talking about various interpretations of literature, and we've found that not everybody will always read the same story the same way. 🎧 It's understood that there are different ways to interpret literature, and, in fact, some works are intentionally written to suggest more than one possible interpretation. **But... let me make something clear.** Although there is no right or wrong way to read a story, your interpretation must come directly from the text. What I'm saying is, sometimes we use our own feelings and beliefs to create meanings that simply aren't there. But the interpretation of literature is like scientific theory in a way... it must be based on facts from the text.

LISTENING PRACTICE 01

p. 59

1. Ⓑ   2. Ⓒ

📋 **NOTE-TAKING**

Purpose: Want to submit essay to writing contest
Major in English?
– No, philosophy.
Essay was written for English course?
– Yes, but I revised it.
⇒ Okay
Topic? – Bronte sisters' novels

Listen to a conversation between a student and a professor.

Professor: Hello. Can I help you?

Student: Hello, Professor Nordstrom. Is it okay if I submit an essay to the English department's writing contest?

P: Oh, certainly. Please have a seat. [pause] You don't look familiar. What's your name?

S: Marilyn Gilmore, sir.

P: Marilyn Gilmore? Q2 🎧 Are you majoring in English?

S: No, I'm not. Actually, I've decided to major in philosophy.

P: Philosophy? Hmm... I see. Um, was your essay written in a course from the English department?

S: Yes, it was originally written for Professor Stein's Introduction to English Literature class last semester. But I've revised it quite a bit since then.

P: Professor Stein's class? Okay. Well, that's fine, then. **If you're not an English major and want to participate in the contest, you need to have taken some English courses.**

S: Great. Here it is.

P: Thank you. And what's the topic of your essay?

S: I wrote about the Bronte sisters, Emily and Charlotte. It's a comparison of their novels.

P: That's an excellent topic. I look forward to reading it.

LISTENING PRACTICE 02

p. 61

1. Ⓓ   2. Ⓑ

📋 **NOTE-TAKING**

Savanna: between tropical rain forest and desert
– warm, rainy (only summer)
– dry winter → water stress of plants & many fires

How plants grow: adaptation
① water: storing in trunks / using long roots / losing leaves
② fire: keeping buds underground & having thick bark

Listen to part of a lecture in a botany class.

Professor: The savanna is another name for tropical grasslands located between a tropical rain forest and a desert. It can be found mostly in the plains of Africa. The savanna is warm all year, and rain falls mostly during the summer. Q2 🎧 In winter, the dry season, it rains very little and plants experience water stress. **Yes, it's the kind of stress you know.** Fires are also common at this time, because the dead, dry leaves burn very easily.

Despite this unfriendly environment, a variety of plants grow in the savanna. So, how do they do it? Adaptation. When there is a drought, they survive by storing water in their trunks and reaching underground water <u>with their long roots</u>. They also save water by, um, by losing their leaves in the winter. Some plants have adapted to <u>deal with fire</u>, as well. Their buds <u>are kept safe</u> underground, and many of the trees of the savanna <u>are protected</u> by thick bark. And others, such as the baobab tree, <u>protect themselves from</u> both fire and drought by storing water in their bark and trunk.

LISTENING PRACTICE 03   p. 63

1. Ⓐ   2. Ⓓ

📋 NOTE-TAKING

Warming-up
– helps avoid <u>injury</u> and should be done <u>before stretching</u>
Q. stretching ≠ warming up?
A. warming up → raise <u>body temperature</u>
   stretching → lengthen muscle
   (without warming up → <u>injury</u>)
   e.g. <u>slow jog</u> or aerobic dance

Listen to part of a lecture in a sports class.

Professor: One of the most important steps in <u>an effective exercise routine</u> is properly warming up. Warming up <u>helps you avoid injury</u> by raising your body temperature, which lets your muscles know that they need to <u>prepare themselves for activity</u>. It should always be done before you start stretching... usually a mild activity such as slowly running in place is best.

Student: Excuse me. Did you say it <u>should be done before stretching</u>? Q2 🎧 <u>I always thought stretching was actually a warm-up activity.</u>

P: Well, some people may call stretching a warm-up. **But we warm up to raise our body temperature, and we stretch to lengthen our muscles**. And you really should warm up before you stretch. Stretching without raising your body temperature could <u>lead to minor injuries</u> to your cold muscles. So before you exercise — and before you stretch — always warm up to get your heart pumping and your blood flowing to your muscles. Either a slow jog or a bit of aerobic dance <u>would be an ideal way</u> to get your body ready.

iBT PRACTICE   pp. 65~66

1. Ⓑ   2. Ⓒ   3. Ⓑ, Ⓒ, Ⓓ   4. Ⓒ

📋 NOTE-TAKING

Unhealthy <u>cycle</u> starts:
– Rising <u>prices</u> mean rising collateral values.
– Banks offer larger <u>loans</u> as collateral values rise.
– People borrows more, increase the demand, drive up prices

Bubble expands:
– Banks lend money even to low-income borrowers
– People buy homes to get <u>rich</u>

Listen to part of a lecture in an economics class.

Professor: Good morning, class. Today, we're talking about debt-driven bubbles in housing prices. When a home buyer borrows money, the house itself serves as collateral for the loan. Hmm ... I don't think you're <u>familiar with</u> that term, collateral. It's a kind of security. If the borrower fails to repay the loan, the bank <u>takes over and sells</u> the house to pay it off.

   Getting back to the point, higher house prices mean <u>higher collateral values</u>. That is, when house prices rise, the collateral values increase; and banks are more willing to lend mortgages. As loans become <u>easier to get</u>, more buyers take out loans, increase the demand for houses, and drive up house prices. Moreover, when house prices rapidly rise, banks <u>relax lending standards</u>. Now, they are willing to lend large amounts of money to people even <u>with very low incomes</u>. Q4 🎧 <u>Meanwhile, people start to borrow more to get profits</u> by reselling houses. They don't need homes and can't actually pay for them. **They only want a piece of the pie, right?** As long as <u>the bubble expands</u>, all houses are increasing in value; all loans are getting paid off. Both lenders and borrowers conclude the risk is low. The bubble <u>grows out of control</u>. And, sooner or later, home values stop increasing. The bubble pops.

S: Why do the home values stop increasing, though?

P: Well, there are many factors, but it's mostly because their real value was <u>never very high</u>. Remember, in this situation, most borrowers can't really pay their loans. If the increase stops or even slows down, there can be a panic and a crash. As we know, the real estate bubble in the United States triggered the 2008 <u>global financial crisis</u>.

VOCABULARY REVIEW

pp. 68~69

A 1. vision   2. easel   3. bark   4. import
B 1. Ⓑ   2. Ⓒ   3. Ⓐ   4. Ⓓ
C 1. drought   2. rain forests   3. Plains
   4. trunk
D 1. Ⓒ   2. Ⓐ   3. Ⓑ
E 1. Ⓒ   2. Ⓐ   3. Ⓑ   4. Ⓐ
F 1. Ⓑ   2. Ⓒ   3. Ⓒ

UNIT
04 Function

BASIC DRILLS 01

p. 71

1-1. Ⓒ   1-2. Ⓑ   2-1. Ⓑ   2-2. Ⓐ

1.

Listen to part of a lecture in an environmental science class.

Professor: Dams are used to produce electricity from flowing water. People generally have a good opinion of them. They think that unlike fossil fuels, dams don't produce large amounts of pollution that causes global warming. So dams are considered to be a clean and environmentally safe way of producing electricity.

However, flooding large areas of land creates a lot of greenhouse gases. As the flooded plants decay, they produce greenhouse gases such as carbon dioxide. In the end, the amounts produced might be the same as those produced by other sources of electricity. Do you understand what I'm saying? It means that dams might play a big part in global warming as well.

2.

Listen to part of a lecture in an economics class.

Professor: The overall tax system in the U.S. is progressive, meaning the percentage of tax tends to increase with increasing income. Those with higher incomes pay more in total taxes and a higher rate of taxes. For example, a person making $100,000 annually might pay 25% of their income in taxes, while someone with an income of $30,000 might only pay 10%.

Student: 🎧 But... rich people might think this is unfair.

P: Yes, they might. But the concept behind the progressive tax system is that people with high incomes should pay more because they can do so without having to give up anything important. I mean... the money they pay in taxes wouldn't be needed to buy basic necessities.

BASIC DRILLS 02

p. 73

| 1-1. Ⓓ | 1-2. Ⓑ | 2-1. Ⓐ | 2-2. Ⓑ |

1.

Listen to part of a lecture in a nutrition class.

Professor: According to a study, most people choose to become vegetarian because they care about animal welfare or because they want to be healthier. Few do so out of concern for the environment. As it shows, people have little understanding of the impact eating meat has on the environment. However, what we eat matters environmentally. Researchers examined 300 randomly chosen diets. They found the food with the highest impact was beef. When they replaced beef with chicken, it dramatically reduced the average carbon footprints of the diets by 54%. In addition, the revised diets showed slight improvements in their Healthy Eating Index scores. Lower-carbon diets can be healthier, too. Practically speaking, eating no meat may not be the best idea, but eating less meat will make a difference.

2.

Listen to part of a lecture in an art class.

Professor: The Barbizon school was a group of 19th century French landscape painters. Instead of classical paintings in which the landscape was nothing more than the background, they created paintings that focused on the beauty of the landscape itself. The Barbizon painters each had their own style and ideas, but they all used nature as the main subject of their paintings. And they painted ordinary scenes of nature, rather than dramatic ones. These paintings showed simple things like the changing seasons or the changing light of the day. It was an informal school, but it played an important role in establishing a new kind of landscape painting as a genre.

LISTENING PRACTICE 01

p. 75

| 1. Ⓒ | 2. Ⓓ |

📋 NOTE-TAKING

How to write a reaction report?
→ write your opinion
not summary?
⇒ summary + interpretation
there is no right or wrong answer

Listen to a conversation between a student and a professor.

Student: Excuse me, Professor Kane. Is it okay if I ask you a quick question?

Professor: Of course, Shaun. Come on in.

S: Thanks. There's something I didn't really understand in class today. Um, could you please explain exactly what you meant by a reaction report? I'm not sure what I'm supposed to write.

P: Q2 🎧 It's quite simple, really. You just need to write your opinion.

S: My opinion? But in class you said that it was a sort of summary.

P: Well, yes. A reaction report should contain a summary of the material. But the most important part is how you choose to interpret it.

S: How should I get started?

P: I'd suggest starting with the summary. After that, you can write your personal interpretation of the material.

S: Got it. I guess I'll give it a try.

P: Great. And relax, Shaun. There's no right or wrong answer when you're writing a reaction report. Just tell me what you think the material means.

S: All right, I will. Thanks for your help, Professor Kane.

LISTENING PRACTICE 02

p. 77

| 1. Ⓑ | 2. Ⓓ |

📋 NOTE-TAKING

The inventor of the telescope
1. Who was the inventor?
– Galileo? No. → used it in astronomy first
– Lippershey. Yes → Galileo improved it

2. Galileo's achievements (with telescope)
① observed the stars
② proved "the Earth moves round the Sun."
⇒ people believe he invented telescope

Listen to part of a lecture in a history of science class.

Professor: The invention of the telescope led to great advances in astronomy. So, do you know who invented it? Galileo Galilei? Actually, Galileo wasn't the inventor of the telescope. He, um... he just introduced and, uh, used it in astronomy for the first time.

The actual inventor of the first telescope was a Dutch eyeglass maker named Hans Lippershey, who combined two kinds of lenses in 1608. Galileo learned of this invention in 1609. Despite never having seen it, he worked out the mathematics of the device and immediately set about improving it. With this new tool, he could observe the stars and made many great discoveries. Observations of mountains on the Moon, stars in the Milky Way, and the moons of Jupiter… these are known as his, um, major achievements. And, importantly, the use of the telescope convinced him of the correctness of the Copernican.theory that "the Sun does not go round the Earth but the Earth rounds the Sun." He really did many great things… and made the telescope famous. So it's not surprising that many people believe that he is the inventor of the telescope.

LISTENING PRACTICE 03　　p. 79

1. 2. Ⓐ

📋 **NOTE-TAKING**

Color-blindness
: not blind to all color, but to certain colors
Cause
cones in the eyes (red, blue, green cones)
If not working or missing
⇒ can't distinguish certain colors

Listen to part of a lecture in a biology class.

Professor: As you probably know, some people are color-blind. But this doesn't mean that they can't see any color at all. It's not as if they're always watching a black-and-white movie. Actually, no one is truly blind to all colors. Rather, color-blind people have trouble seeing the difference between, um… between certain colors. **Q2** 🎧 To understand what causes color-blindness, you need to know about the cones in your eyes.

Student: *[surprised]* There are cones in my eyes?

P: Yes, there are, but they're very small. They're actually a type of cell located at the back of your eye on your retina. Different cones are sensitive to different colors. You need three types of cones to properly see colors: red cones, blue cones, and green cones. If any of these cones don't work properly or are missing, your brain won't be able to distinguish a certain color from another. For example, a green leaf might look gray, or a blue car might look silver. But you would still be able to see the full range of other colors.

1. Ⓓ 2. Ⓐ 3. Ⓓ 4. Ⓑ

📋 **NOTE-TAKING**

Symbiosis
: special relationship between different organisms

Types of symbiosis
① both benefit (e.g. ants and acacia plants)
② one benefits, the other isn't affected (e.g. orchids and tree)
③ one benefits, the other is harmed (e.g. flea and cat)

Listen to part of a lecture in a biology class.

Professor: Sometimes in nature you find two organisms that have a special relationship. One organism — or both — needs the other to, uh, to survive. This is called symbiosis. Um, the word symbiosis basically means "living together."

There are a few different forms of symbiosis. The first type of symbiosis involves two species that both benefit from their close relationship. Here's an example: Have you ever seen an acacia plant covered with ants? The ants get sugar and stems to live in... and acacia plants get protection because the ants defend the plant from attackers. See how this kind of symbiosis works? Both the ants and the acacia plants are, um, happy with the situation.

The next kind of symbiosis is similar, but instead of both species benefiting, only one species does. The other isn't affected at all. Orchids are an example of this kind of symbiosis. See, in rain forest, orchids grow on other plants, usually on the branches of tall trees. Orchids benefit by being on tall trees because they get a lot more sunlight. Plus, their seeds travel further when they fall from way up high. The trees don't get anything out of the symbiosis, but they aren't harmed, either.

The last type of symbiosis is where one species benefits and the other is harmed. An example would be a flea on a cat. **Q4** 🎧 The flea is happy because it gets to feed on the cat's blood. **And... how about the cat? Is the cat happy, too?** This relationship is... good for the fleas but bad for the cats.

A 1. income   2. organism   3. convince
     4. impact   5. correctness
B 1. Ⓒ   2. Ⓑ   3. Ⓓ
C 1. ecosystem   2. moons   3. decay
     4. doubt
D 1. Ⓒ   2. Ⓐ   3. Ⓒ
E 1. Ⓒ   2. Ⓑ   3. Ⓐ
F 1. Ⓐ   2. Ⓓ   3. Ⓒ

Actual Practice Test 2

01   pp. 88~89

1. Ⓐ   2. Ⓓ   3. Ⓒ   4. Ⓑ   5. Ⓐ

📋 **NOTE-TAKING**

About the literary magazine
Be my adviser
– But I'm busy
Need professional advice so I don't fail again
– Okay. Choose the title?
Not chosen yet → Do not use university name
⇒ Bring your ideas next week

Listen to a conversation between a student and a professor.

Professor: Oh, hello Kevin. Come on in. Now, what did you want to see me about?

Student: Well, it's about the new student literary magazine I'm starting up. The college has agreed to publish it, and I've found several classmates willing to volunteer as editors and proofreaders.

P: That's great. It's very ambitious of you.

S: Thanks. But now I need to find an adviser for the magazine. Would you be interested? I think you're the perfect choice.

P: Well, I'm sorry, but right now I'm spending all my free time working on a book I've been writing.

S: *[disappointed]* Oh, really? But it wouldn't take up much time. You'd just need to look things over once in a while.

P: To be honest, Kevin, I wouldn't be comfortable putting my name on the cover of a magazine unless I had the time to put a 100% effort into it.

S: I guess I understand. It's just that this will be my second attempt at starting a literary magazine. The last one failed to win any awards because I didn't get the proper advice from professional writers... like you.

P: I see. Well, I suppose I could help you out from time to time.

S: I'd really appreciate it. I admire your writing style so much. I'm sure with your help this magazine will be a success.

P: I hope so. By the way, have you chosen a title for it yet?

S: Not yet. I want to choose something special that will get people's attention. Q5 It seems like college magazines these days all have the same boring titles.

P: I know what you mean. **They all use the name of their**

university. The Wisconsin University Magazine... The Magazine of New York College...

S: Exactly. Anyway, I have some ideas for a title. I just need to select the best one.

P: Why don't you come back next week and bring your ideas with you? We can discuss how you can make this magazine something special.

S: That's great! I'm so glad you're going to help us. I promise it won't be too much of a burden.

P: I'm sure it won't be. I'll see you next week, then.

02

pp. 90~91

6. Ⓑ 7. Ⓐ 8. Ⓑ 9. Ⓐ

📋 NOTE-TAKING

Life without rules
= the state of nature

Hobbes – negative view like "war"
          fight against everyone
How to avoid?
– Setting rules called "Social Contract".
– Everyone agrees to follow it

Listen to part of a lecture in a philosophy class.

Professor: Good afternoon, class. I have a question for you. What would you do if there were no rules? Would you skip work or classes? What do you think other people would do? In my opinion, it's really hard to imagine what life would be like without rules.

Actually, the idea of life without rules is something that lots of philosophers have wondered about. They have a special term for it: the state of nature. The state of nature... it's basically just a situation — an imaginary situation — where there are no rules. No laws. And people do whatever they want. Understand?

One of the most famous philosophers who wrote about this idea, about, um, the state of nature, was Thomas Hobbes. He lived in England during the, the 17th century. Hobbes had a pretty negative view of the state of nature. Uh, he imagined that without rules people would treat each other badly. According to Hobbes, they'd live alone, be mean to others, and fear everyone else. They'd do whatever they had to do to stay alive. You know what? He actually said that the state of nature would be just like war. A war where every person was fighting against every other person.

Q9 🎧 It's a pretty awful point of view, isn't it? I don't know about you, but I wouldn't want to live like that,

and neither would have Hobbes. I can tell because Hobbes did have an idea about how to avoid the terrible problems of the state of nature. He said there had to be a set of rules. These rules would be able to create peace. And, um, they'd help people out a lot. Help them get along with one another and, um, work together. He called these rules a "social contract." A social contract is like a set of rules that everyone in a society agrees to follow... because the rules will help keep order. Got it? So, to summarize: the philosopher Thomas Hobbes thought that if humans lived in a state of nature, they'd be bad and mean... and the way to prevent people from behaving that way was with the use of a social contract that everyone would agree to follow.

BASIC DRILLS 01   p. 95

1-1. (A)   1-2. (1) connotation (2) denotation
2-1. (A)   2-2. (1) F (2) F

1.

Listen to part of a lecture in a linguistics class.

Professor: A word, any word, has a meaning. That's how we know what the word expresses. But the meaning of every word has two different parts. First, there is its "denotation." This is the meaning that you can find in the dictionary. Second, there is the word's "connotation." This goes beyond what the word expresses. For example, you can find the meaning of the word "home" in the dictionary. That is the word's denotation. The connotation, however, is different. What comes to mind when you think of "home?"
Student: I think of warmth and love.
P: Very good. Warmth and love are part of the connotation of the word "home."

2.

Listen to part of a lecture in a physics class.

Professor: Newton's law of gravity is still used, but it doesn't explain why gravity exists. In 1915, Einstein offered a new theory of gravity. He showed that gravity is a result of the curving of space rather than an attractive force.
    I'll give you an analogy. Imagine a bowling ball pressing down on a trampoline. The surface of the trampoline would curve downward instead of being flat. Now imagine placing a lighter ball at the edge of the trampoline. What will happen? It will roll down toward the bowling ball. This attraction to the bowling ball occurs because the trampoline curves downward, not because the two balls are actually attracted to one another by an invisible force. That's the way gravity works. Mass creates a depression in space, so it pulls everything toward itself. The heavier the mass, the harder it pulls.

BASIC DRILLS 02   p. 97

1-1. (B)   1-2. (A)   2-1. (C)   2-2. (A)

1.

Listen to part of a lecture in a biology class.

Professor: Humans have about 200 types of cells. All of these cells contain approximately 20,000 identical genes. Genes are small sections of DNA that code for proteins. However, each cell type has a different set of chemicals that determines which genes get used. These chemicals attach to the genes and turn them "on" or "off." As a result, the genes are expressed differently, which creates different types of cells. These "epigenetic changes" do not change the DNA sequence; instead, they affect how cells read the genes. In fact, everything around us triggers chemical changes that affect gene expression, including diet, age, and stress levels. This explains why genetically identical twins can exhibit different behaviors, skills, health, and achievement. However, epigenetic changes are not permanent. Our appearance, health, and personality can all change in response to our surroundings.

2.

Listen to part of a lecture in a history class.

Professor: Thousands of years ago, ancient Egyptians were making paper using the papyrus plant. They would gather this plant, which grew along the Nile River, and remove the outer part of the stem. Then they would cut the rest of the stem into long, thin pieces and put it in water for several days to remove the sugar. The next step was to lay these pieces on top of one another. And this would allow the remaining sugar to stick them together like glue. Another layer would be added on top, and then the two layers were pounded until they stuck together. After the papyrus was allowed to dry and polished with a rock, it was ready to be used as paper.

LISTENING PRACTICE 01
p. 99

1. C 2. B

📋 **NOTE-TAKING**

The endocrine system
- Communication system in body
- Produce hormones & regulate body
Q. Nervous system for communication?
A. Both are for communication but work differently
  - Nervous system ≒ telephone: one to one
  - Endocrine system ≒ radio broadcast: one to everyone

Listen to part of a lecture in a biology class.

Professor: The endocrine system is used by the body for communication. It's a group of organs that produce hormones and use them to send messages. By traveling through the blood stream, these hormones can affect the activities of cells throughout the body. They help regulate a variety of things, such as growth and eating... even the way you feel.

Student: But, um... isn't the nervous system responsible for communication in the body?

P: You're right. Both systems are used for communication, but they work in different ways. Think of the nervous system as a telephone network. Messages are sent from one cell to another, one at a time. But what if you wanted to communicate with a large group of people all at once? Calling each of them one at a time would take too long. But if you owned a radio station, you could broadcast a message that everyone could hear at once. This is sort of how the endocrine system works. It doesn't produce radio waves, of course, but it sends hormones throughout the body in much the same way.

LISTENING PRACTICE 02
p. 101

1. D 2. B

📋 **NOTE-TAKING**

Red dwarf stars
- Small (100 times smaller than the Sun)
- Long life (burning fuel slowly)
- Why red?
  Because of low temperature
  Like colors of a fire (blue > yellow > red)

Listen to part of a lecture in an astronomy class.

Professor: Looking up into the night sky, all of the beautiful stars look pretty much the same to you and me. But the scientists who study these stars divide them into groups based on their similarities and differences. Red dwarf stars, for example, are the most common type of star. Compared to other stars, they're quite small... they range in size from about a hundred times smaller than the Sun to only a couple of times smaller. Red dwarfs last a very long time, since they burn their fuel very slowly. And... well, does anyone know what makes red dwarf stars red?

Student: Is it because they're so hot?

P: No... But that's a pretty good guess. The answer is related to temperature, but red dwarf stars are actually cooler than most other types of stars. Think about the colors of a fire. The hottest part of a fire, which is nearest to the source of fuel, glows blue. The middle part is yellow, and the coolest part of a fire, on the outer edge, glows red.

LISTENING PRACTICE 03
p. 103

1. B 2. Close-up – B / Long shot – C / Medium shot – A

📋 **NOTE-TAKING**

Shot sizes in films
; how much scene is shown
- Directors choose the right one for a situation
  (like using crayon for drawing)
① Close-up: shows face (tension)
② Long shot: shows large area (situation)
③ Medium shot: shows body language (power & importance)

Listen to part of a lecture in a film studies class.

Professor: Directors have many visual tricks they use to express feelings in their films. One of these is the size of their shots... that is to say, how much of the scene is shown within the frame. Shot size is an important tool for creating the proper mood, and directors must choose the correct one for each situation. You know... you might use a crayon to draw a picture, but you wouldn't use one to take your notes, would you?

Okay, a close-up, which shows nothing but an actor's face, can be used to create tension. A long shot, on the other hand, will show a large part of the area surrounding the actors, perhaps a city street or forest. It doesn't create a strong mood like a close-up, but it can help the audience better understand a situation. Finally, a medium shot shows the actors from a comfortable distance that is similar to the way we usually view things. It's not great for facial expressions, but can easily show an actor's body language. Also, the position of the actors in a medium shot can also be used to show power or importance.

iBT PRACTICE

1. Ⓓ   2. Ⓒ   3. Ⓐ   4. Ⓒ

📋 **NOTE-TAKING**

Q. Heat up a pan to 100 ℃ and add a drop of water?
– evaporate because it's the boiling point
Q. Heat to 200 ℃?
– evaporate faster?
No. The drop would stay ⇒ Leidenfrost effect
above 160 ℃(= Leidenfrost point) bottom of the drop
becomes steam
∵ Steam prevents heat transfer
  → Water drop takes longer to evaporate

Listen to part of a lecture in a physics class.

Professor: Okay, here's the situation: you're in the kitchen and you heat up a frying pan to 100 degrees Celsius. What would happen if you placed a single drop of water onto the pan? Anyone?

Student: Um... it would bubble for a second, and then it would be gone. It would evaporate.

P: That's correct. It's because the boiling point of water is 100 degrees Celsius. Q4 🎧 So, what do you think would happen if we heated the pan up to 200 degrees and then placed the drop of water on it?

S: It would evaporate twice as fast?

P: **Well, you may think so, since it's twice as hot as the boiling point. But in reality, you would see a different picture.** The drop would stay on the surface of the pan for up to 20 seconds before it, um, evaporated. This is something called the Leidenfrost effect, named after the scientist who discovered it. Here's what happens... if the surface of the pan is hot enough, usually somewhere above 160 degrees Celsius, we say that it has passed the Leidenfrost point. At this temperature, the bottom of the water drop will quickly turn into a gas, becoming steam. This steam will prevent the heat from moving from the pan to the upper part of the water drop. I mean... um, because of the steam, the process of heat transfer is slowed down. As a result, the water drop takes longer to

evaporate, even in temperatures higher than the boiling point. It may sound strange, but it's true!

VOCABULARY REVIEW

A 1. polish   2. mood   3. predict   4. glow
B 1. Ⓒ   2. Ⓐ   3. Ⓓ
C 1. responsible   2. director   3. layers
   4. analogy
D 1. Ⓐ   2. Ⓓ   3. Ⓒ
E 1. Ⓑ   2. Ⓒ   3. Ⓐ   4. Ⓒ
F 1. Ⓑ   2. Ⓑ

Connecting Content

BASIC DRILLS 01 p. 111

1-1. The North Atlantic – Ⓐ, Ⓒ / The Pacific and Indian oceans – Ⓑ, Ⓓ 1-2. Ⓐ
2-1. Ⓓ – Ⓑ – Ⓐ – Ⓒ 2-2. (1) vs (2) euil

1.

Listen to part of a lecture in an Earth science class.

Professor: The global conveyor belt is a system of ocean currents that transport water around the world. While winds primarily drive surface currents, deep currents are driven by thermohaline circulation. At the poles, cold ocean water becomes saltier and denser from ice formation. The dense water sinks, and then surface water moves in to replace it, thus creating a current. The conveyor belt begins in the North Atlantic. Cold water flows deep in the ocean to the south and resurfaces in the Pacific Ocean or Indian Ocean. As cold water warms and rises, it brings carbon dioxide and nutrients to the surface. It supports the plankton and algae that form the base of the world's food chain. Now, the water travels in surface currents back to the North Atlantic. It takes 1,000 years to complete a circuit.

2.

Listen to part of a lecture in a historical linguistics class.

Professor: The English language has undergone a lot of changes over time. For example, "u" and "v" were different forms of the same letter hundreds of years ago. At the start of a word, the "v" form was used, while the "u" form was used everywhere else. So, in those days, a word like "love" would have been spelled l-o-u-e, instead of l-o-v-e. There was, however, no difference in the sounds the two letters made until the 18th century. At that time, the "v" form began to sound like [v] and the "u" form as [u]. When they were first separated, the letter "v" was put before "u" in the alphabet, although this order was later reversed.

BASIC DRILLS 02 p. 113

1-1. Ozone layer – Ⓐ, Ⓒ / Ground-level ozone – Ⓑ, Ⓓ 1-2. Ⓐ 2-1. Opera – Ⓑ, Ⓓ / Operetta – Ⓐ, Ⓒ 2-2. Ⓑ

1.

Listen to part of a lecture in an environmental science class.

Professor: Whether ozone gas is "good" or "bad" depends on where it is in the air. Good ozone, in the upper atmosphere, is the same as the ozone layer. This ozone blocks dangerous UV rays and protects life on our planet. Ozone becomes "bad" when it gets too close to the surface. Air pollution is the greatest cause of surface-level "bad" ozone. Bad ozone causes smog and can lead to serious health problems, including lung disease. It can also cause less serious, but still dangerous, health problems like coughing and throat pain. The smog created by ground-level ozone can also limit the growth of trees and crops.

2.

Listen to part of a lecture in a music history class.

Professor: In the 18th century, opera was very popular among the higher classes. These operas usually had tragic stories and, importantly, they were only sung in Italian. Solo artists performed most of the songs, instead of choruses or groups of singers. Among middle-class people, however, the operetta was more popular. Operettas weren't as serious as operas... in fact, they were often quite funny. And, unlike operas, they were sung in the audience's native language.

Student: I guess that helped people understand the stories better.

P: Of course. So, in an operetta, the characters could communicate directly with the audience. Also, operettas often had choruses that would sing along with the star performers.

LISTENING PRACTICE 01

p. 115

1. Ⓑ   2. Yes – Ⓐ, Ⓒ, Ⓓ / No – Ⓑ, Ⓔ

NOTE-TAKING

Purpose: photocopy the book on reserve
→ You have a book that hasn't been returned
I'll return it tomorrow & pay the fine
Photocopy?
→ Fill out the form

Listen to a conversation between a student and a librarian.

Student: Hi. I need to make some photocopies from one of your books on reserve.

Librarian: All right. Can you let me know the name of your professor and the class that this is for?

S: Sure. It's for Professor Jacob's History of East Asia class.

L: Okay. And can I see your student ID, please?

S: Here you are.

L: Thank you. Hold on one moment, please. *[pause]* Hmm... I'm sorry, but you seem to have a book that hasn't been returned yet. You already owe a $2 fine. If you don't return it this week, you'll have to pay twice as much.

S: Oh yeah! Sorry. I promise I'll return it tomorrow and pay the fine. Um, does this mean I can't make photocopies from the book on reserve today?

L: No, you still can. But you'll have to fill out this form first.

S: Sure, no problem.

L: And, let's see... You said it was for Professor Jacob's class? The History of East Asia?

S: That's right.

L: Is this the book that you're looking for?

S: That's it. Thanks so much for your help.

LISTENING PRACTICE 02

p. 117

1. Ⓑ   2. Federal government – Ⓐ, Ⓒ /
State governments – Ⓑ, Ⓓ

NOTE-TAKING

U.S. governments
State governments (= 13 colonies governed themselves)
: weak → created federal government
⇒ Federal & state governments share power
Federal: money system, international trade, military
State: local business, elections, public health & safety

Listen to part of a lecture in a politics class.

Professor: America's first form of government was based on individual state governments. You know, America originally consisted of 13 colonies, and these colonies governed themselves. However, it was soon discovered that these state governments were too weak to rule effectively. Instead, it was decided to create a federal government. The federal government controls the entire country. However, it shares its powers with each of the state governments.

Let me give you some examples. It would be too confusing if each state had a different form of money, so the federal government controls a single form of money that is used by all the states. The federal government is also in charge of things like international trade and the military. State governments, on the other hand, control local business, conduct elections, and are responsible for public health and safety. So, as you can see, power in America is shared between the federal and state governments.

LISTENING PRACTICE 03

p. 119

1. Ⓓ   2. Yes – Ⓐ, Ⓒ / No – Ⓑ, Ⓓ

NOTE-TAKING

Weathering
: big rocks → sand & soil
Causes of physical weathering
① Water: ice creates cracks
② Salt: creates pressure
③ Temperature: rocks get larger in heat
⇒ break apart

Listen to part of a lecture in a geology class.

Professor: Who can tell me where sand and soil come from? *[pause]* The answer is "weathering." Weathering turns big rocks into little rocks, and little rocks into sand and soil. You need to know that there are two types of weathering, but we're only going to look at one today: "physical weathering." Um, in this type of weathering, the rocks don't change chemically, only physically. That is, big rocks get smaller, and little rocks turn into even smaller rocks.

There are many causes of physical weathering, but the most common is water. Water enters holes and cracks in rocks. During very cold weather, the water turns into ice, which creates more cracks. Salt is another leading cause of physical weathering. Water often has some salt in it. After the water dries up, the salt remains. The salt creates pressure on the rocks. Changes in temperature also cause physical weathering. Rocks get slightly larger in the sun and heat, then return to their normal size when it gets cooler. This damages rocks and will eventually cause them to break apart.

iBT PRACTICE

1. Ⓓ   2. Ⓒ – Ⓐ – Ⓔ – Ⓑ – Ⓓ   3. Ⓑ

📋 NOTE-TAKING

Leaning Tower of Pisa
Started to lean when first 3 floors were finished
Built next 3 floors parallel with the ground
Started to lean to the south / 2 more floors built
Holes made in base of tower and filled with cement
Added earth to the south, then removed earth from the north

Listen to part of a lecture in an architecture class.

Professor: Many tourists visit Italy to see a tower that looks like it's falling over. Of course, I'm talking about the Leaning Tower of Pisa. Construction on the tower began in 1173.

Student 1: Um… when did it start to lean?

P: Good question. Finishing the first three floors took five years. This is when the tower started leaning. After that, work stopped for 100 years. In 1275, a new team of builders took over. In order to fix the lean, they built the next three floors parallel with the ground instead of with the other floors. But the tower started leaning the other way, toward the south. Nevertheless, they finished the tower in 1350, and even then it was still leaning. It was left alone for a long time, but it was eventually going to fall over. So, in 1934, to strengthen the foundation, workers made holes in the tower's base and filled them with cement. Unfortunately, this caused the tower to lean more. In 1995, workers started adding earth under the south side, to raise it. But they realized that this was making it lean more too, so they stopped. Finally, in 1999, they tried the opposite idea, and removed earth under the north side. This worked out well, and the tower was made 16 inches straighter.

Student 2: Professor… why didn't they just make it perfectly straight?

P: Well, they could have. But then all those tourists who go to see the Leaning Tower of Pisa would have been pretty upset, right?

VOCABULARY REVIEW

A   1. govern   2. dense   3. parallel
4. reverse
B   1. Ⓓ   2. Ⓐ   3. Ⓒ
C   1. perform   2. fine   3. throat   4. upset
5. leading
D   1. Ⓒ   2. Ⓑ   3. Ⓐ
E   1. Ⓐ   2. Ⓐ   3. Ⓒ   4. Ⓒ
F   1. Ⓑ   2. Ⓓ   3. Ⓓ

UNIT
07 Inference

BASIC DRILLS 01

p. 127

1-1. Ⓑ 1-2. Ⓑ 2-1. Ⓓ 2-2. (1) T (2) F

1.

Listen to part of a lecture in an art class.

Professor: This next painting is by Jackson Pollock. Pollock invented a style called action painting. He'd take a large canvas, perhaps as big as an entire wall, and lay it down on the floor. And then he... well, his method of painting made use of his entire body. He'd dip sticks into paint and use them to throw the paint onto his canvas as he walked around it. 🎧 Some said his paintings should be laid down in galleries because Pollock put them on the floor when he painted them. **But think about it... after you take a picture of the sky overhead, you don't display it on the ceiling to appreciate it.**

2.

Listen to part of a lecture in a botany class.

Professor: So, let's talk about tulips. I'm sure you're all familiar with tulips, right? But does anyone know where they come from?
Student: They come from the Netherlands, don't they?
P: 🎧 I knew you would say that. I'm sure many of you thought tulips are native to the Netherlands. But nothing could be further from the truth. Tulips actually originated in Turkey. In fact, their name comes from the Turkish word for turban. They were brought to the Netherlands in the 16th century, where they quickly grew popular. These days, as I'm sure you know, the people of the Netherlands grow many tulips and export them to other countries all around the world.

BASIC DRILLS 02

p. 129

1-1. Ⓑ 1-2. Ⓐ 2-1. Ⓐ 2-2. Ⓑ

1.

Listen to part of a lecture in a geology class.

Professor: The Earth has four layers: the crust, the mantle, the outer core, and the inner core. 🎧 How do you think geologists have figured this out? **Digging? Nice try, but the Earth is 4,000 miles from surface to center.** Anyone else? Okay... then I'll tell you. Geologists use seismic waves. This is not a direct method, like digging, but it works better, and you don't sweat as much! Seismic waves pass through the Earth during earthquakes. When they pass through different materials, their direction, motion, and speed change quite a bit. By studying seismic waves, scientists have learned about the four major components that make up the Earth.

2.

Listen of part of a lecture in an anthropology class.

Professor: Europeans arrived in the Americas in 1492. This started a global transfer of plants, animals, and diseases known as the "Columbian Exchange." New crops and animals altered diets, lifestyles, and the economy in the New World and the Old. Corn and potatoes became a major food in many countries and led to huge population growth in the Old World. To the New World, Europeans brought pigs, cows, chickens, and horses, as well as crops like sugar cane, wheat, bananas, and coffee. Massive demand for new crops worldwide, especially sugar, coffee, tobacco, and cotton, created new patterns of production and new global networks of trade.

🎧 The Columbian Exchange also had some unintentional disastrous results, such as the spread of disease. This tragic aspect was one-sided leading to the death of millions of Native Americans.

LISTENING PRACTICE 01 p. 131

1. Ⓒ 2. Ⓐ

NOTE-TAKING

Problem: Late for the exam!
→ You can't go inside
Want to meet professor to reschedule the exam
→ Stop by at 12:30
    But you must get permission from the dean for
rescheduling

Listen to a conversation between a student and a teaching assistant.

Student: *[out of breath]* Oh no! Please don't tell me the exam has already started.

Teaching Assistant: I'm sorry, but it has. You're nearly 15 minutes late.

S: I know. My alarm didn't go off this morning. Can I go inside, please?

A: I'm sorry, but you know the rules. Once the exam starts, nobody is allowed to enter the classroom.

S: *[sadly]* Yes, I know. I guess I need to speak to Professor Griffin about this. When do you think I can meet with him?

A: Stop by his office around 12:30.

S: All right, I will. Do you think he'll allow me to reschedule my exam?

A: Oh. I'm afraid that's not up to him. You'll have to get permission from the dean of the department.

S: Really? Oh boy... Do you think the dean will let me reschedule the exam for later this week?

A: To be honest, the dean is quite strict when it comes to school policy. You're going to have to work pretty hard to convince her.

S: Well, I guess I have to try. Wish me luck...

A: Good luck. I hope it all works out.

LISTENING PRACTICE 02 p. 133

1. Ⓒ 2. Ⓑ

NOTE-TAKING

Contrast Effect
: evaluating the same thing differently accd. to reference
e.g. ① hands in cold & hot water → warm water
    ⇒ feel different
② bad one next to good one
    ⇒ good one looks much better
③ $1,000 vs. $150
    ⇒ $150 looks much cheaper

Listen to part of a lecture in a psychology class.

Professor: We'd like to believe we always make reasonable decisions. Unfortunately, it's not true. One of the reasons we can't decide properly is the contrast effect. We tend to evaluate the same thing differently according to reference items. For example... um, imagine you put your left hand in cold water and your right in hot water. And then you put both hands together into warm water. You know what you'll feel, right?

Student: My left hand will feel hot, but the right will feel cold.

P: Yes. Each hand feels different even though they are in the same water. This kind of thing often happens. Let's see... have you ever noticed how salespeople use the contrast effect? They put a poor quality product next to one that they want to sell in order to make the target product look much better. Q2 🎧 Or they show you a $1,000 shirt first and then a $150 shirt. You are likely to buy the second one because it seems very cheap compared to the first one. **But the truth is... the hot water has tricked you again.**

LISTENING PRACTICE 03 p. 135

1. Ⓓ 2. Ⓓ

NOTE-TAKING

Limestone cave formation
begins with rain and CO_2 in the air → become acidic
→ absorbed by soil (more CO_2 from dead plants)
→ acidic water dissolves limestone (large space develops)
→ water washes away rock & sand
→ cave is formed

Listen to part of a lecture in a geology class.

Professor: Take a look at this amazing photograph of a limestone cave. Did you ever wonder how this kind of cave forms?

Surprisingly, it begins in the air... specifically, it begins when two things work together in the air — rain and carbon dioxide. As rain falls from the sky, it absorbs carbon dioxide in the air, which causes it to become acidic. When this rain reaches the earth, it is absorbed by the soil, where it takes on more carbon dioxide that has been produced by dead plants. If this water passes through any limestone in the ground, it can form caves. What happens is that the acidic water has a chemical reaction with the limestone. The water dissolves the limestone, causing large spaces to develop.

And that's not all water does. As the space in the limestone grows, underground water can flow through these areas, washing away loose rock and sand. This causes the space to enlarge even further. All of this occurs over the course of hundreds of thousands — perhaps even millions — of years, and eventually a cave is formed.

iBT PRACTICE   pp. 137~138

1. Ⓓ 2. Ⓐ 3. Ⓑ 4. Ⓒ

📝 **NOTE-TAKING**

Here for appointment to arrange class schedule
Performance: 4.0 GPA
Know about honors program? – Have heard about it
Rigorous, do not like to push students into it
But many benefits, especially for graduate school
Main thing is the thesis:
– 30 pages
– Often meet with honors advisor
– Senior year, present and defend thesis
Students must join or not by the beginning of sophomore year
Take time to think about it, meet again later

Listen to a conversation between a student and an advisor.

Student: Ms. Lewis? Hi, I'm here for my appointment.

Advisor: Oh, hi, Peter. We need to arrange your class schedule for the fall, right?

S: That's right.

A: Good. And I see you have a 4.0 GPA. Very nice!

S: Yeah. I'm pretty happy about it.

A: You should be. I want to ask you something. Do you know about the honors program here?

S: Um... I've heard about it. Do you think I should apply?

A: Hmm... Well, it is rigorous. As an advisor, I don't like to push students into it. But it has a lot of benefits. It's especially good if you want to go to graduate school.

S: Oh, I didn't know that. But it's more difficult?

A: It's quite a bit more work. The main thing is your thesis. It needs to be 30 pages. And, well, the standards are high. You'll have to have frequent meetings with an honors advisor. There is one for every major. In your senior year, you'll need to present and defend your thesis. Now, even normal classes are demanding. And this is a step up.

S: I see.

A: It's a challenge, but here's the thing. Q4 🎧 Students have to apply by the beginning of their sophomore year. And, um, and it would affect which classes you could take.

S: Ah, okay. Can I take some time to think about it?

A: Yes, that's what I was going to suggest. Think it over for a day or so. Then we can meet again and talk about class registration.

S: Okay, that sounds good.

VOCABULARY REVIEW   pp. 140~141

A 1. reschedule 2. alter 3. hunter
   4. arrange
B 1. Ⓑ 2. Ⓐ 3. Ⓓ
C 1. sweat 2. target 3. earthquake
   4. defend
D 1. Ⓐ 2. Ⓐ 3. Ⓓ
E 1. Ⓒ 2. Ⓑ 3. Ⓐ 4. Ⓒ
F 1. Ⓐ 2. Ⓒ

Actual Practice Test 3

01

1. Ⓑ 2. Ⓑ, Ⓒ 3. Ⓐ 4. Yes – Ⓑ, Ⓓ / No – Ⓐ, Ⓒ

📋 NOTE-TAKING

The Industrial Revolution
- Why it started in Great Britain
① Geography: natural resources
             harbors & waterways
② Social situation: labor forces in cities ↑
             ∵ new farming technology
             → farmers lost jobs and went to cities
③ Political & economic conditions:
  - No war in GB
  - Protecting inventors' rights & good banking system

Listen to part of a lecture in a history class.

Professor: We already know that the Industrial Revolution brought about some, um, really big economic and social changes all over the world. We also know the main cause of the Industrial Revolution was the development of new technologies. But what I want to discuss today is why the Industrial Revolution started in Great Britain, not somewhere else.

There are three factors that explain why it started in Great Britain: geography, the social conditions in Great Britain at that time, and the economic and political situation there.

Let's consider the geography of Great Britain. It had a number of natural resources like iron, coal, um, lead... and so on. With these raw materials, Great Britain had no trouble, um, developing its new industries like steel production. And another geographical advantage Great Britain had was a lot of harbors and waterways. It was possible to move goods around the country very easily. Having so many harbors and rivers made it easy to move goods abroad, too.

A second important factor was the social situation in Britain at that time. Well, socially, Great Britain's labor force was growing and moving to the cities. This was because new farming technologies were being developed. This helped people get more food and led to an increase in Great Britain's population. But at the same time, these new technologies took away the jobs of many farmers and left them unemployed. Without any other options, um, farmers went to the cities and became the workers that — that made the Industrial Revolution possible.

The last factor I wanted to mention was the political and economic conditions in Great Britain. First of all, there was no war in Great Britain. So, stable political and economic conditions had been established. The British government encouraged new technological developments by protecting inventors' rights. The government also tried to avoid regulating the economy... um, rather, they made a good banking system to help factory owners borrow money and open new factories easily. These turned out to be very helpful policies that contributed to the success of the Industrial Revolution.

02

5. Ⓒ 6. High salinity – Ⓐ / Low salinity – Ⓑ, Ⓒ, Ⓓ 7. Ⓐ 8. Ⓑ

📋 NOTE-TAKING

Some parts of the ocean are saltier than others
(average salinity = 35,000 ppm = 3.5% salt)
Why?
① Evaporation → salinity ↑ (e.g. tropical oceans)
② Precipitation → salinity ↓
③ Addition of fresh water → salinity ↓
④ Ice melting → salinity ↓ (e.g. polar oceans)

Listen to part of a lecture in an oceanography class.

Professor: What is one main difference between seawater and fresh water? Seawater is salty, of course. Interestingly enough, though, not all seawater has the same salinity — the same salt content. Some parts of the ocean are saltier than others. I should start off by explaining that salinity is usually expressed in ppm, parts per million, and the average salinity of seawater is 35,000 ppm.

Student: Parts per million? Could you explain what that means?

P: Sure. It's a way of measuring the amount of one substance in relation to another: in our case, that would be salt to water. It means that out of a million parts of water, 35,000 parts are salt. Another way to think of it is to divide 35,000 by a million and you get 3.5%. So seawater is 3.5% salt.

Q8 🎧 Anyway... let's talk about the salinity of seawater again. As I was saying, it varies. So what is it that causes the salinity of seawater to vary by

174

region? Well, there are a lot of factors, like evaporation, precipitation, the addition of fresh water from rivers, and the melting of ice. These processes may either increase or decrease the salinity of seawater.

Let's start by considering evaporation. It's the process that turns liquid water into a gas. And when that happens in the ocean, water gets removed, but all the salt stays behind. So the result is that evaporation increases the salinity of seawater. In general, tropical places that experience a lot of evaporation have oceans with high salinity.

Now, precipitation is basically the opposite of evaporation. When it rains, more water gets added to the ocean, but the amount of salt stays the same. What this means is that precipitation decreases the salinity of seawater. Fresh water flowing to the ocean from rivers has the same effect as precipitation. It introduces water but not salt... so it causes the salinity of seawater to decrease. Near the coast, seawater often has a lower salinity because of the flow of fresh water from rivers. Lastly, there's melting ice, which also introduces fresh water into the ocean. The result, again, is to lower the salinity of seawater. This is obviously more of a factor in polar oceans.